POWER PLAYS

Dramatic Short Plays for Student Actors

Laurie Allen

Meriwether Publishing
A division of Pioneer Drama Service, Inc.
PO Box 4267
Englewood, CO 80155

www.pioneerdrama.com

Editor: Debra Fendrich
Cover design: Devin Watson
Interior design: Melissa Nethery
Project manager: Karen Bullock

© Copyright 2016 Meriwether Publishing

Printed in the United States of America
First Edition

Library of Congress Cataloging-in-Publication Data

Allen, Laurie, 1962- author.
  Power plays : dramatic short plays for student actors / by Laurie Allen.
    First edition
  Englewood, CO : Meriwether Publishing, a division of
    Pioneer Drama Service, Inc., [2016]
  Includes bibliographical references and index.
  LCCN 2016015231
  ISBN: 9781566082075 (pbk. : alk. paper)
  LCSH: Young adult drama, American.   Teenagers – Drama.
  LCC PS3601.L4324 P69 2016
  DDC 812/.6–dc23 LC record available at https://lccn.loc.gov/2016015231

1   2   3   16   17   18

CONTENTS

Performance Application

About the Author

SEASHELLS

SYNOPSIS: Old high school friends, including one who lost his eyesight in an explosion in Iraq, have their ten-year reunion at a beach.

CAST: 3M, 2F
    Mark (late 20s)
    Brett (late 20s)
    Seth (late 20s)
    Cassie (late 20s)
    Jenna (late 20s)

SETTING: Beach
PROPS: Sunglasses, seashell, engagement ring

A group of high school friends who haven't seen each other in several years have planned a reunion at a beach. MARK and BRETT, both barefoot and wearing sunglasses, are looking out over the audience as if facing the ocean. MARK is blind, having lost his eyesight in an explosion in Iraq.

MARK: What color is it?

BRETT: The ocean's blue. You know that.

MARK: It smells green.

BRETT: Well, maybe it is a bit green.

MARK: I want to step closer and feel the water on my feet.

BRETT: *(Takes his arm.)* Just a few more steps forward.

MARK: *(Steps forward.)* Thank you. It's warm. Emerald green.

BRETT: You're right. *(Small laugh.)* You must have eyes in your toes.

SETH: *(ENTERS.)* Hey, Mark! You came! We weren't sure if you'd show up.

MARK: Wouldn't miss it for anything. Our ten-year reunion?

BRETT: Mark, it's Seth, in case you weren't sure.

MARK: I know. I recognize the voice.

SETH: Of course you do! Bill will be here in a few hours. Man, he's going to be so stoked to see you! I mean, you guys have been best friends since when?

BRETT: Third or fourth grade, right?

MARK: Third grade. But we haven't seen each other since my accident in Iraq.

BRETT: So are you doing okay, Mark?

MARK: *(Anxious to change the subject.)* Yeah, I'm doing great.

CASSIE: *(ENTERS.)* What a great place for our ten-year reunion! This beach is gorgeous!

SETH: Cassie! *(They hug.)*

BRETT: Great to see you, Cassie! *(They hug.)*

CASSIE: Hi, Mark. I'm sorry about the accident. I heard it was an explosion.

MARK: Hey, Cassie, yeah. The bomb went off just a few yards away from me.

CASSIE: *(Hugs him.)* I'm so sorry.

MARK: You don't have to feel sorry for me. I'm doing well.

CASSIE: I see that. I mean...

MARK: *(Small laugh.)* No pun intended, right?

CASSIE: I'm sorry.

MARK: Don't worry about it.

SETH: Hey, Mark, have you talked to Jenna yet?

MARK: No. Not yet.

CASSIE: She's here. I remember how you two used to be like this. *(Crosses fingers.)* Inseparable.

SETH: That was back in high school.

CASSIE: Past high school. You were still together during your tour in Iraq, weren't you?

MARK: We were. Up until the accident.

BRETT: Okay, change of subject here.

MARK: *(Feels a seashell on the sand with his toes, bends over, and picks it up.)* I doubt if Jenna's ready to see me.

CASSIE: Uh, you know she's engaged now, don't you?

MARK: No, I didn't.

CASSIE: Yeah, she's got quite a ring on her finger.

MARK: *(Drops the seashell.)* Where'd she meet him?

SETH: She met him at work. At some accounting firm. I think she's a receptionist there.

MARK: Did she bring him?

CASSIE: No. She said he was in New York for some meeting.

SETH: Mark, when did you last talk to Jenna?

MARK: It's been a couple of years. *(Takes a deep breath.)* I smell rain.

CASSIE: I don't smell it, but the clouds seem to be moving in. *(Looks over MARK'S shoulder.)* There she is.

BRETT: Jenna? Where?

CASSIE: She's over there by the volleyball net.

MARK: What is she wearing?

CASSIE: A sundress and a floppy straw hat.

MARK: What color is her dress?

CASSIE: Kind of an orange. Maybe peach. Something like that.

MARK: Does she look the same? Is her hair still long?

SETH: No. It's shorter. Shoulder length.

BRETT: But she still looks the same. At least I think so.

SETH: Hey, Mark. There are a lot of beautiful women on this beach. Lots of gorgeous fish in this sea.

BRETT: Yeah, like that white bikini chick over there. Shall we head that way and start up a little small talk? Looks like she has some friends too.

CASSIE: *(Annoyed.)* Knock it off. You two haven't changed a bit.

MARK: I'd rather talk to Jenna. Cassie, would you ask her to come over here, please?

CASSIE: Sure. I'll go get her.

MARK: Thanks. *(CASSIE EXITS.)*

SETH: Are you sure you're up for this?

MARK: Sure, why wouldn't I be?

SETH: Man, you've just been through so much. The war. The explosion. Do you really want to face Jenna and hear about her engagement to some stupid accountant?

MARK: I need to do this.

BRETT: Why? Why put yourself through more agony?

MARK: I want to congratulate her.

SETH: I don't get it. Why should you be so nice to her after she bailed on you when you needed her most?

MARK: It wasn't like that.

SETH: Oh, no? Looked that way to me. To everyone else too.

MARK: My tour in Iraq was hard on both of us. The separation. The unknown.

SETH: Losing your eyesight.

MARK: Yeah. I'd rank that as the worst day of my life. Not losing my eyesight, but losing all those buddies of mine in the explosion. That was the worst.

BRETT: I can't even imagine.

MARK: You know, I'd do it all over again.

SETH: I don't get how you can say that.

MARK: I was proud to serve our country. Wish I still could.

SETH: You're a true hero. A better man than me, that's for sure.

MARK: No. Not me. My friends who lost their lives… they're the heroes.

BRETT: It cost you plenty too. Your eyesight. *(Pause.)* And Jenna. You guys belonged together.

MARK: If Jenna's happy, then I'm happy.

SETH: After what she did to you? *(Shakes his head.)* Amazing. You know, you should tell her what a pathetic person she was for leaving you during the worst time of your life.

MARK: *(Firm.)* I said it wasn't like that. That's not how it happened.

SETH: Why don't you just give Jen a quick hello, then we'll go introduce ourselves to the little white bikini over there. I'll give you a detailed description as we head that way.

BRETT: Sounds like a good plan to me.

MARK: No. I need to talk to Jenna. It's important that I do this.

SETH: Well, get ready 'cause she's coming this way with Cassie.

MARK: How does she look?

SETH: Honestly? Nervous.

BRETT: She does look nervous.

MARK: Is she pretty?

BRETT: Yeah, I guess so. I guess you could say she's still pretty.

SETH: Pretty with shorter hair.

CASSIE: *(ENTERS with JENNA.)* Look who's here.

JENNA: Hi, guys.

SETH: Hey, Jenna.

JENNA: Hey.

SETH: Good seeing you again, Jenna.

JENNA: You too, Seth. How have you been, Brett?

BRETT: Good.

JENNA: And you, Mark?

MARK: Good. *(A long awkward pause.)*

CASSIE: Who's up for volleyball?

BRETT: Me!

SETH: Me too. Let's go. *(CASSIE, BRETT, and SETH EXIT.)*

MARK: *(After a pause.)* Hello.

JENNA: Hello. Those three haven't changed a bit.

MARK: No, I guess they haven't.

JENNA: Cassie said you really wanted to see me. *(Realizes her word choice.)* Oh! I'm sorry. I didn't mean to say it that way. Cassie said you wanted to say hello.

MARK: You don't have to be careful with your words. See me. Talk with me. We both know what it means. It's fine.

JENNA: Thanks. So... how have you been?

MARK: Fine. And you?

JENNA: Good. I'm working at an accounting firm.

MARK: So I heard. I also heard you're engaged.

JENNA: Yes. He's a junior partner at the firm.

MARK: Congratulations. He's a lucky guy. *(Pause.)* It's been two years since we've talked.

JENNA: I know. Since everything changed for us. And yet... it seems like just yesterday that we were walking along the beach. Holding hands. Laughing. In love. *(Bends over and picks up the seashell that MARK was holding earlier.)* Picking up pretty seashells. *(Looks at the seashell, then places it in MARK'S hand.)* This one's pretty.

MARK: *(Feels it.)* Yeah, I saw this one earlier.

JENNA: You saw it?

MARK: With my hands.

JENNA: I still have all the seashells that we picked up.

MARK: *(Hands her the seashell.)* Add this one to your collection.

JENNA: Thank you. *(Pause.)* This is hard, Mark. Did you have something you wanted to say to me?

MARK: Yes.

JENNA: What?

MARK: Congratulations. On your engagement.

JENNA: *(Looks at her ring.)* Oh. Thanks.

MARK: Can I feel it?

JENNA: What?

MARK: The ring. I assume he gave you one.

JENNA: Yes, of course you can touch it. *(Touches MARK'S hand with her left hand.)*

MARK: *(Feels her ring.)* It's big.

JENNA: Yeah, I guess it is.

MARK: What's his name?

JENNA: Chris.

MARK: Jenna and Chris. That sounds good. Do you ride bikes along the boardwalk?

JENNA: No.

MARK: Dance in the moonlight?

JENNA: No.

MARK: Stare at the stars until you can't keep your eyes open.

JENNA: No.

MARK: Collect seashells?

JENNA: No.

MARK: Good.

JENNA: Good?

MARK: Those were our things.

JENNA: Yes.

MARK: Do you love him? Never mind. Of course you love him.

JENNA: Of course.

MARK: But do you love him… like you loved me?

JENNA: It's different.

MARK: Good.

JENNA: You know what we had was one-of-a-kind.

MARK: Yeah, everyone always said we belonged together. Brett even said so today.

6

JENNA: And did you tell him that it was you? Have you told anyone that you're the one who broke up with me?

MARK: Sort of... no, not really.

JENNA: Why not? To make me look like the bad one?

MARK: No, not at all!

JENNA: But it was you.

MARK: Yes.

JENNA: It was all you.

MARK: Yes.

JENNA: You left me in tears. Heartbroken.

MARK: Yes.

JENNA: You know I would've—

MARK: You would've stayed with me.

JENNA: I wanted to stay.

MARK: *(Smiles.)* You're not heartbroken now.

JENNA: No. But a piece of me died when you broke up with me.

MARK: When's the wedding?

JENNA: Next fall probably. We haven't set the date yet.

MARK: May I come? Am I invited?

JENNA: No.

MARK: What's this? You won't invite an old friend to your wedding?

JENNA: You aren't my old friend. You were my love. My best friend. My soul mate.

MARK: What am I now?

JENNA: A stranger.

MARK: No, Jenna. You still know me better than anyone.

JENNA: Do I?

MARK: I haven't changed.

JENNA: But I have.

MARK: Yes. Yes. You've lost something.

JENNA: So have you.

MARK: Sure, I lost my eyesight. But you lost your sparkle. And that laugh. I also don't hear that excitement in your voice. I guess maybe it's still there, but I'm just not the one who gets to hear it now.

JENNA: I grew up. I'm not that silly naïve girl who names stars after her future children anymore.

MARK: That's too bad.

JENNA: Stop it. You're upsetting me.

MARK: Jen, I'm sorry. It's just... I've missed you.

JENNA: And I'm still angry at you. I begged you to let me stay with you. For us to work through this together. I didn't care that you could no longer see. I loved you with all of my heart. But no. You dismissed me as if I were a soldier in the army. Dismissed!

MARK: You didn't need to waste your life with a blind man.

JENNA: Waste my life?! I never thought that for a minute!

MARK: I spared you the pain.

JENNA: *(Angry.)* You didn't spare me any pain! You caused me pain! You were so angry about being blind that you convinced yourself that I could never be happy with you. You were so smart, weren't you? So smart! But you were wrong, because the truth is... *(Chokes back tears as her anger turns to heartbreak.)* ...the truth is... I will never be truly happy without you.

MARK: Aren't you happy now?

JENNA: *(Twists the ring on her finger.)* I settled for a different kind of happy.

MARK: Settled?

JENNA: Chris and I are two mature people. We're making financial decisions together regarding our future. Looking for a house. Planning how many children we will have.

MARK: Do you write their names in the sand?

JENNA: No.

MARK: Write your own names in the sand?

JENNA: No.

MARK: *(Squats down and writes in the sand.)* M plus J. Remember?

JENNA: What's the point of remembering?

MARK: *(Writes.)* Equals love.

JENNA: Equaled love.

MARK: *(Stands.)* Jenna... I'm sorry.

JENNA: For the record, I would've stayed with you forever.

MARK: For the record, I wish I had let you.

JENNA: You do?

MARK: Yes. I was so wrong to let you go.

JENNA: *(Twisting her ring while looking at the seashell she holds in her left hand.)* So, um... thanks for the seashell.

MARK: We both found it. So it's perfect for your collection.

JENNA: Yes. *(Looks up at MARK.)* Mark?

MARK: Yes?

JENNA: I've missed you too.

MARK: Jenna...

JENNA: Yes?

MARK: Do you want to meet me here tonight?

JENNA: Tonight? Here? Why?

MARK: I thought we could lie on a blanket and look at the stars like we used to do. For old time's sake. Do you want to? You can describe them to me. *(Points up.)* "Look at that one! That's the brightest star out here tonight. I think I'll name it Thomas." And I'll say, "Look at that one! It's twinkling just like your eyes. I think I'll name it Jenna."

JENNA: *(Small laugh.)* You always named them after me.

MARK: Yes. All the stars are you. Beautiful. Glowing. Spectacular. Hopeful.

JENNA: *(Deep breath.)* Yes. I'll meet you here tonight.

MARK: You will?

JENNA: Yes.

MARK: Jenna?

JENNA: Yes?

MARK: Are you as happy as before? Are you as happy with Chris as you were with me?

JENNA: How could I be? You were my everything.

MARK: As you were mine.

JENNA: See you tonight.

MARK: See you. *(JENNA EXITS.)*

OBSESSION

SYNOPSIS: A college freshman realizes that her roommate suffers from anorexia.

CAST: 2F
Maddie (18)
Destiny (18)

SETTING: Dorm room
PROPS: Desk, chair, two sweaters, backpack, textbooks

MADDIE stands as if in front of a full length mirror in her dorm room.

MADDIE: *(Puts her hands on her waist and twists around as she stares disapprovingly at herself and talks to her reflection.)* Ugh! I hate the way you look. Who has ever seen such a huge waist? It's disgusting. *(Pinches her waist.)* You're disgusting, Maddie. Disgusting with a big capital D. You've got to do something. Something more. Less. Less calories. Or no calories. No calories would be good. Maybe that would help. Fill up more on water. That doesn't have any calories. No more cheating going over eight hundred calories a day like you did yesterday. Try for even less. Like today. An apple and three saltine crackers. Not bad. *(Grabs her waist.)* But it's not working! Look at all this fat! Oh, I hate it! Why do I have to look so disgusting? I've got to cover it up! *(Grabs a bulky sweater off the chair, throws it on, and wraps it tightly around her.)*

DESTINY: *(ENTERS carrying a backpack. Notices MADDIE wearing a sweater.)* Hi, Maddie. You cold?

MADDIE: Hey, Destiny. A little.

DESTINY: I knew it.

MADDIE: Knew what?

DESTINY: That you're getting sick. This is great. Just great! We're roomies, so your germs become my germs. I don't have time to be sick. Too much to do!

MADDIE: Don't worry. I'm not sick.

DESTINY: I heard you in the bathroom last night.

MADDIE: What do you mean?

DESTINY: Throwing up.

MADDIE: Sorry. It was probably just something I ate. Dorm food is the worst.

DESTINY: Really? You're fine now?

MADDIE: Yeah.

DESTINY: Oh, sure. You're probably just like me.

MADDIE: How's that?

DESTINY: Denying it. I can be running around with a fever of a hundred and one, and I'm like, "No, I'm not sick! I refuse to be sick." And then it hits me. I can't put one foot in front of the other, and I crash. Hard. So that better not be what you're doing. *(Opens her backpack on the desk.)* I have tons of studying to do.

MADDIE: Me too.

DESTINY: So, if you are sick, please, please just keep your germs on that side of the room. *(Takes out a book and sets it on the desk.)* First, I've got to study for a biology quiz tomorrow. *(Takes out another book.)* Then I have to read a chapter for my lovely humanities class and write a three-page paper.

MADDIE: Sounds delightful.

DESTINY: Yeah, charming. Therefore, I must be clear of germs and remain healthy so I might study my life away. Please promise me you're not sick.

MADDIE: I'm not sick. I promise.

DESTINY: You're lying, aren't you?

MADDIE: No. Really. I'm not sick.

DESTINY: But it's eighty degrees outside, and you're wearing a bulky sweater. You probably have a fever. *(Touches MADDIE'S forehead.)* Hmmm… you don't feel hot.

MADDIE: I told you. I'm not sick.

DESTINY: Wait, you're not pregnant, are you? I've noticed you haven't been eating much the last few weeks.

MADDIE: God, no! How could you think that? I don't even have a boyfriend.

DESTINY: Okay, good. Best news I've heard all day. I guess you're just one of those chronically cold people. *(Takes out another book.)* Have I mentioned lately that I hate calculus?

MADDIE: Not since this morning.

DESTINY: Just to make it clear, I hate calculus.

MADDIE: Even thinking about it hurts my head.

DESTINY: Welcome to my world.

MADDIE: Hey, I could use a little sympathy too. I have to read two chapters about time management and goal setting. Real exciting, huh?

DESTINY: That would put me to sleep.

MADDIE: Welcome to my world.

DESTINY: *(Sits at desk and opens a book.)* I'd rather sleep than study. But we're in college. We're not supposed to sleep, right?

MADDIE: No kidding. I mean, I'm tired all the time. *(As DESTINY studies, MADDIE takes off the sweater and goes back to the mirror and stares at herself some more. After a moment, DESTINY glances up and watches her for a moment.)*

DESTINY: Why do you always do that?

MADDIE: What?

DESTINY: Stare at yourself in the mirror. I've noticed you do that like a million times a day.

MADDIE: *(Not looking at DESTINY.)* Because I hate how I look. I'm so fat. How can someone have such a disgusting waist? *(Grabs her waist.)* I wish I could do lipo or find a way to cut all this fat off.

DESTINY: Fat? Are you kidding me?

MADDIE: *(As if staring at her profile the mirror.)* My stomach is huge. Oh, I hate it!

DESTINY: Whoa! Reality check. Where are we?

MADDIE: *(Looks at Destiny.)* What?

DESTINY: Where are we?

MADDIE: In our dorm room.

DESTINY: Right. But you're acting like we're at some carnival fun house. You know, with those mirrors that distort how you look so you're really tall and skinny or short and super fat?

MADDIE: Super fat pretty much sums it up.

DESTINY: My God, believe me, you look great! You've even lost some weight, I can tell. Here, the rest of us are fighting off the evil "freshman fifteen," and you're losing weight.

MADDIE: *(Turns back to the mirror.)* I know what I see in the mirror. I'm fat. I'm thinking... maybe if I cut down to five hundred calories a day.

DESTINY: That's not healthy! No wonder you're tired all the time! You need food for energy. How can you possibly study when you're hungry?

MADDIE: I can do it. It's called will power.

DESTINY: No, it's called stupid. Come on, you need to stop obsessing over your waist size. Who cares if you're a size five or a size zero? You look great.

MADDIE: I know what I see. My waist is disproportionate to the rest of my body.

DESTINY: No, it's not.

MADDIE: Yes, it is! *(Turns to DESTINY.)* Look! Look at me!

DESTINY: What? You look amazing! I wish I could fit into all your tiny, super-cute clothes!

MADDIE: This is not amazing! *(Pinches waist.)* Can you not see this?

DESTINY: See what?

MADDIE: *(Puts the sweater back on.)* You're lying. Or just being polite. *(Grabs a second sweater to put on.)*

DESTINY: What are you doing?

MADDIE: Covering up. I don't want anyone to see me.

DESTINY: Seriously? You're really going to walk around in eighty-degree weather wearing two sweaters?

MADDIE: Maybe.

DESTINY: And go to your classes looking like that? Like some incredible hulk minus the green color and muscles?

MADDIE: I already look like that! That's the problem!

DESTINY: What's really going on here?

MADDIE: I look disgusting! That's what's going on.

DESTINY: No, there's something else.

MADDIE: You wouldn't understand. No one does.

DESTINY: What I do understand is that you're obsessed with the way you look.

MADDIE: So?

DESTINY: So... why don't you tell yourself you look great instead of filling your mind with all that negative talk. *(Mocking.)* "I'm fat. My waist is huge. I look disgusting. Have you ever seen anyone as disgusting as me?"

MADDIE: Stop it!

DESTINY: I'm sorry, but you need to get over yourself.

MADDIE: *(Turns back to the mirror.)* How can I when I look like this? Maybe if I do something more drastic. Like stop eating all together.

DESTINY: Have you lost your mind? If you stop eating, you'll die.

MADDIE: Worry about yourself. I just need to figure out a way to lose more weight, because whatever I'm doing now isn't enough.

DESTINY: You're a nut case. You need to get some help.

MADDIE: You're the one who needs help. Not me! Like I said, worry about yourself. What I need is another sweater. *(Looks around the room in a panic.)*

DESTINY: Stop it! It's hot outside!

MADDIE: I don't care. I don't want anyone to see me looking like this.

DESTINY: Seriously, you need to talk to a counselor at the health center.

MADDIE: Why? Is a counselor going to help me lose weight so I don't look so... *(Looks at herself in the mirror.)* ... so disgusting?

DESTINY: No, but I know the counselor will help you.

MADDIE: How? By helping me learn to cope with my ugliness?

DESTINY: Oh my God, really? You've got to stop this! Look, I realize we've only known each other for a month, but I see things. I see you stare at yourself in the mirror for hours! Then you become frustrated and sad. But you have to listen to me. What you see isn't real. It's all in your head.

MADDIE: Don't pretend that you know me, because you don't!

DESTINY: I know that you barely eat.

MADDIE: So what? I'm dieting. What college girl doesn't diet?

DESTINY: Me.

MADDIE: Then you're the weird one!

DESTINY: Me? You're the one who barely eats and now is talking about never eating again!

MADDIE: I was joking.

DESTINY: And then there's the constant exercising.

MADDIE: So?

DESTINY: So, you get up at five o'clock every morning and go out jogging for what seems like hours. And then, if you have any energy left, you're doing sit-ups until you collapse.

MADDIE: So what?

DESTINY: So what? It's not normal. Then last night... you throwing up in the bathroom. I bet it wasn't the first time.

MADDIE: I told you, it was something I ate!

DESTINY: No, it was BECAUSE you ate!

MADDIE: Stop it!

DESTINY: What? Were you afraid you'd gain a pound after eating a meal?

MADDIE: Just drop it!

DESTINY: You say you're disgusting? Listening to you puke is disgusting!

MADDIE: I told you, I was sick!

DESTINY: You're not sick. You even said so. You were puking up your guts because you think you're fat. Admit it.

MADDIE: Leave me alone.

DESTINY: Why are you doing this to yourself? Obsessing over an imaginary flaw? You're not fat. Believe me when I tell you this. You. Are. Not. Fat.

MADDIE: Yes, I am!

DESTINY: You've got to stop saying that.

MADDIE: I need to lose weight!

DESTINY: You need to be thinking about college life beyond classes. You know, like clubs and boys. No one cares what you weigh, I promise.

MADDIE: I care.

DESTINY: Seriously, you need to talk to someone. You know, get some help.

MADDIE: Why? You think I'm a mental case? *(Silence.)* Oh, please! I'm sure you don't like every part of your body.

DESTINY: You know what? You're right. I don't. I don't like my teeth. They're not straight. But I don't obsess over it. I don't stare in the mirror for hours and hours agonizing over my crooked teeth. And I don't stop smiling. Or eating. Or socializing with my friends because they may notice my teeth.

MADDIE: Well, you're not me!

DESTINY: No. But you do all those things. You obsess. You stare. And except for classes, you pretty much spend all your time either exercising or staring in the mirror. It's robbing you of enjoying your freshman year. *(Silence.)* I really think you should talk to someone about it. I'm sure the health center has some great counselors.

MADDIE: I don't need anyone to talk to. I just need to lose more weight. Then maybe—

DESTINY: Then what? You'd be happy?

MADDIE: Maybe.

DESTINY: *(To herself.)* Why me?

MADDIE: Why you what?

DESTINY: Why do I have to get a roommate who doesn't know how to have fun? Who is obsessed with one thing and one thing only? The size of her waist. The fat she imagines that surrounds her body. The fat that only exists in her mind, but for some unimaginable reason, causes her to puke her guts out if she eats a few bites of food. Yeah, why me?

MADDIE: Geez! Sorry you got stuck with me.

DESTINY: You know, I was hoping for a roommate who would stay up late at night with me, eating pizza, studying, laughing. Maybe even becoming great friends. But you don't laugh. You don't eat. *(Moves to the mirror.)* You just stand here in front of this mirror and stare at yourself. Telling yourself that you're fat, which you're not. But you don't believe me. I don't know. Maybe...

MADDIE: What?

DESTINY: If you don't get help, I should ask to change rooms.

MADDIE: What? You don't want to be my roommate anymore?

DESTINY: And listen to you puke?

MADDIE: I'm sorry. I'm sorry! I can't help myself.

DESTINY: I want a roommate who I can have fun with. Someone I can laugh with. Someone who's not falling apart on the inside.

MADDIE: *(Turns to the mirror. A pause.)* I am falling apart, aren't I?

DESTINY: You need to get some help, Maddie. You need to figure out how to be happy. As I say, crooked teeth and all.

MADDIE: I do want to be happier. *(Pulls the sweater around herself tighter.)* And I do feel like I'm missing out on life. Meeting new people and having fun at parties. *(Looks at herself in the mirror.)* But instead, I stay in here. Alone most of the time.

DESTINY: Then why don't you talk to one of the health center counselors?

MADDIE: I don't know...

DESTINY: Come on, I'll go with you. Just make an appointment. It's the first step. We all need help at times.

MADDIE: I don't want to always be like this. Hating myself all the time.

DESTINY: Then let's go to the health center.

MADDIE: And you won't ask for a new roommate?

DESTINY: Not if you'll reach out for some help.

MADDIE: All right. I will.

DESTINY: Good. And I'm here to help you too.

MADDIE: Thanks.

DESTINY: Come on. Let's go. And afterwards, let's blow off studying and catch open mic night at the coffee shop.

MADDIE: But I've got to study.

DESTINY: Not tonight, Maddie. Not tonight. Tonight we're going to have some fun. *(They EXIT.)*

FIRE

SYNOPSIS: A young woman wants to break up with her physically abusive boyfriend and move out.

CAST: 1M, 1F
   Blake (30)
   Ashley (late 20s)

SETTING: Apartment living room
PROPS: Couch or loveseat, lighter

BLAKE and ASHLEY are in their apartment after another typical fight. But this time, ASHLEY has had enough. She is holding her neck, and it's obvious that BLAKE was physically abusive.

BLAKE: Say something. *(Pause.)* Come on. Say something. What is this? Are you giving me the silent treatment? *(Pause.)* So you're not going to talk to me now? I said I was sorry. Did you hear me? *(Sarcastically.)* I'm sorry! *(Pause.)* Stop it, Ashley. Stop acting like a two-year-old and get over it! *(Pause.)* Didn't you hear me? I said stop it! *(Pause.)* Baby, I'm sorry. Can't we move on? *(ASHLEY shakes her head.)* Why are you saying no? I'm sorry I lost my temper. Okay? *(Reaches out to touch her, but she recoils.)* Come on, Ash. It'll never happen again. I promise.

ASHLEY: Don't touch me!

BLAKE: Ashley, don't do this. Come on. *(Takes a step closer.)* Let me give you a hug.

ASHLEY: I said, don't touch me!

BLAKE: *(Uses his index finger to poke her arm.)* Touched you.

ASHLEY: *(Steps back.)* You know what, Blake? I'm done.

BLAKE: What do you mean, "you're done"? Done fighting? Okay. Me too. No more fighting. Cross my heart.

ASHLEY: Yeah, I'm done fighting. I'm done with you.

BLAKE: *(Halfway laughs.)* No, you're not. Let's go grab some dinner and put all this behind us. I'll take you wherever you want to go. Chinese. It's your favorite.

ASHLEY: No. I mean it this time. It's over.

BLAKE: Babe, you know we love each other. Let's get past this and move on. I said I was sorry. Can't you accept my apology?

ASHLEY: I accepted your apology the last time. You swore it would never happen again. Just like the time before. And the time before that. You've given me that line, like, a million times.

BLAKE: Ash, you've got to give me another chance. Please? I swear. I really swear this time it'll never happen again.

ASHLEY: I want to hear you say it.

BLAKE: Say what?

ASHLEY: Say what you did to me. I want to hear you say it out loud.

BLAKE: Okay. *(Shrugs.)* I lost my temper.

ASHLEY: That's not what you did to me. Admit what you did.

BLAKE: I just did, Ashley. I admitted that I lost my temper. Okay? Are we good now? Can I give you a hug?

ASHLEY: A hug? Are you kidding?

BLAKE: Come on, Ash.

ASHLEY: No! I never want you to touch me again!

BLAKE: *(Steps forward.)* Baby, come on.

ASHLEY: Stop! Don't you dare come near me!

BLAKE: I'm stopping, I'm stopping. You need to calm down and relax. Take a chill pill.

ASHLEY: Say it.

BLAKE: I already said it. I'm sorry.

ASHLEY: No. Say what you did.

BLAKE: I said that too. I lost my temper. And again, I'm sorry.

ASHLEY: No! Say it!

BLAKE: Say what?

ASHLEY: Say, "I hit you, Ashley!" "I threw you across the room." "I…" *(She holds back tears.)* "…choked you." It's always something to hurt me. But you never admit it.

You call it "losing your temper." You call hitting, slapping, punching... *(Puts hands to neck.)* ...choking... you call that "losing your temper"?

BLAKE: I just pushed you. I didn't hit you. You're overreacting, like you always do.

ASHLEY: A push? You slammed me against the wall! And then you put your hand around my throat... *(Holds back tears.)* I could barely breathe!

BLAKE: That's because you were all over the place. I was trying to calm you down.

ASHLEY: And then you said... *(Holds her hand out to demonstrate him choking her.)* "I can kill you! Do you know that?"

BLAKE: *(Shakes head.)* I don't remember saying that.

ASHLEY: *(Caresses her throat.)* Yes, I know you can kill me. You've threatened to do it before.

BLAKE: I just lose my temper and say stuff. You know I wouldn't really do anything like that.

ASHLEY: Don't give me that shit. When you finally let go, you hit me in the back like I was your punching bag. I'm sure it's already bruised. It hurt, Blake. It hurt real bad. Just like all the other times. Do you even care that you hurt me? Do you?

BLAKE: Ash, come on. Let's put all of this behind us and go have dinner. Sweet and sour pork? Sound good? It's your favorite.

ASHLEY: Dinner? Really?

BLAKE: Yeah. Let's go eat. Like I said, you pick the place. Anywhere you want to go.

ASHLEY: I'm going to my mom's house.

BLAKE: Your mom's? Baby, no, we need some quiet time together. Then I can tell you how much you mean to me. I love you. You mean the world to me, and honestly, I don't know what I'd do without you.

ASHLEY: Well, you're about to find out, because I'm leaving.

BLAKE: Please don't leave. I'd miss you. You know that.

ASHLEY: Well, you better get used to it.

BLAKE: Come on. Don't leave.

ASHLEY: And if I do? Are you going to hit me in the back as I walk out the door?

BLAKE: No, Ash. I'm never going to do that again. I promise.

ASHLEY: Do what again?

BLAKE: You know.

ASHLEY: Say it! Say what you do to me!

BLAKE: Ash, come on...

ASHLEY: Say it!

BLAKE: Stop it, Ash.

ASHLEY: Say, "I beat up my girlfriend!" Say it!

BLAKE: No! *(He raises his hand then quickly puts it down.)*

ASHLEY: Look at you! *(Starts toward door.)* Lie to yourself, but you can't lie to me. Because I know the truth now. *(Stops and looks at him.)* And so do you. You just won't admit it to yourself. Or to me. Goodbye, Blake. *(Continues toward door, but BLAKE blocks her.)*

BLAKE: Ashley, wait! Please! Please don't go! I'll do anything. Anything.

ASHLEY: Let me make this perfectly clear for you. I'm leaving. No more chances. Every time this happens you swear that you're going to change, but you don't. You plead, you beg, and sometimes you even try crying. But your empty promises are just that. Empty. I can't believe you anymore. *(Tries to get around him.)*

BLAKE: No, you're not leaving!

ASHLEY: Oh, yes I am!

BLAKE: *(Grabs her arm.)* I listened to you so now you're going to listen to me.

ASHLEY: *(Pulls away.)* Don't you touch me! I'm not listening to you, Blake. I've heard enough of your lies.

BLAKE: Shut up! Just sit down and shut up! You're going to hear me out!

ASHLEY: No. *(He pushes her down on the couch.)*

BLAKE: If you leave me...

ASHLEY: What?

BLAKE: You'll be sorry. I promise you, you'll be sorry.

ASHLEY: I'm already sorry for staying with you this long. I should have left after the first time you hit me. I should've left you then. But stupid me had a soft spot for your pathetic whining and fake tears. I thought you could change. I thought I could change you.

BLAKE: Listen to me!

ASHLEY: No! I'm leaving!

BLAKE: No, you're not! Because if you do...

ASHLEY: What? What will you do?

BLAKE: I'll... I'll set it all on fire.

ASHLEY: What? My clothes? My stuff? Go ahead. That's all replaceable. It's my self-worth and dignity that aren't.

BLAKE: You leave me, and it all goes up in smoke. I'll set this entire house on fire! Don't believe me? Try me!

ASHLEY: You're evil! You bastard!

BLAKE: A little lighter fluid drenched on the furniture, your clothes... and everything else! *(As if lighting a match.)* Kabooooom! *(Small wave.)* So long...

ASHLEY: *(Glaring.)* If you do anything like that, I'll set you on fire!

BLAKE: *(Smirks.)* Face it, you're stuck with me.

ASHLEY: I'm not doing this. I refuse to be controlled by you for one more day.

BLAKE: You love me and you know it. So why don't you admit it? Let me hear you say it. Come on. Say it. Say it!

ASHLEY: No.

BLAKE: Say it. Say, "I love you, Blake."

ASHLEY: I thought I did, but I was wrong. Love doesn't demand, control, scream, hit... But you do all those things. You don't know the first thing about love.

BLAKE: Oh, yeah? And what do you know?

ASHLEY: Love should be kind. But you're cruel. It should be understanding. But you blame and accuse. It should be easy. But with you, it's difficult. And it hurts. It hurts, Blake, and I'm tired of hurting.

BLAKE: Well, boo-hoo!

ASHLEY: So typical.

BLAKE: Oh, look at my whiney girlfriend here. *(Girl's voice.)* "If things don't go my way, then I get mad and accuse my boyfriend of being abusive." Boo-hoo. Well, look here,

Ashley. I'm not having some stupid girl walk all over me and try to control me. That's not the way it's supposed to work.

ASHLEY: *(Points to him then back to herself.)* THIS is not the way it's supposed to work! This isn't love.

BLAKE: We go along and everything is great. We hang out on the sofa, watch movies, throw popcorn at each other, laugh, and then you get into one of your moods, and there you go. You turn psycho. Ranting and raving about who knows what. And you can never let things go. Never. Like the other day when I left my shoes in the hallway.

ASHLEY: I asked you nicely to pick them up.

BLAKE: And I forgot. So you started nagging. Nag, nag, nag, nag, nag!

ASHLEY: No. I just asked you once more to please put your shoes in the closet.

BLAKE: Nag, nag, nag, nag, nag!

ASHLEY: And what did you do?

BLAKE: *(Matter of fact.)* What did I do? I told you to stop your nagging.

ASHLEY: Yeah, you told me all right. As you screamed and hit my head with your shoe.

BLAKE: *(Shrugs.)* Your fault. You should've shut up.

ASHLEY: I should've left you a long time ago.

BLAKE: Then go!

ASHLEY: I am. I really am this time.

BLAKE: Good riddance!

ASHLEY: My thoughts exactly. *(Starts toward the door.)*

BLAKE: Don't forget what I said!

ASHLEY: What?

BLAKE: I'm going to set it all on fire! Your clothes. Your pretty little trinkets. That ugly stuff you hang on the walls. Everything! So, say goodbye, Ashley. It's all going up in smoke!

ASHLEY: *(Glaring at him.)* Goodbye, Blake.

BLAKE: I'm going to do it! Do you hear me?! I'm going to do it! *(Digs into his pocket.)* Look! I already have the lighter. I'll start right here. *(He holds the lighter next to the couch.)*

ASHLEY: *(Rushes over. Grabs his arm.)* Stop it!

BLAKE: Hey, I'm trying to start a fire.

ASHLEY: Stop it! I mean it! Stop it! *(Grabs the lighter.)*

BLAKE: Why does it matter? If you're not here...

ASHLEY: Why can't we just have a normal breakup? Why can't you just accept that it's not working between us and move on? I'm not happy. You're not happy. All we ever do is fight. Then you get mad and you—

BLAKE: Don't say it! I'm warning you!

ASHLEY: You yell, you threaten, you scream. And you hit. You hit me, Blake.

BLAKE: I told you not to say it!

ASHLEY: And now this? You're threatening to burn the house down. Why can't you control yourself?

BLAKE: *(Grabs the lighter back and holds it up.)* I have all the control in the world. And you're powerless.

ASHLEY: Not anymore. I'm tired of being powerless and weak. Leaving you gives me more power than you can imagine. And I gain something back.

BLAKE: What?

ASHLEY: Myself. I get myself back. Because somehow, between your manipulation, your control, and your smacking the shit out of me, I forgot who I was.

BLAKE: Sure, you go find yourself. I'll be here setting it all on fire. Go for it!

ASHLEY: Then do it. And you'll get thrown in jail, and you can just rot. Yeah, that sounds good.

BLAKE: I'm warning you! If you leave, you'll be sorry.

ASHLEY: No. I'll be sorry if I don't leave.

BLAKE: *(Holds up lighter again.)* Don't think I won't!

ASHLEY: Go ahead. Deal with the consequences. *(EXITS.)*

BLAKE: Get back here, Ashley! I said, get back here! You'll be sorry if you don't! I promise you, you'll be sorry! *(Lighting the lighter.)* I'll burn it all to the ground! Do you hear me? I'll burn it all to the ground!

THE PARK BENCH

SYNOPSIS: An elderly woman suffering from Alzheimer's doesn't recognize her daughter or grandchildren, who are trying to take her home from the park.

CAST: 1M, 3F
  Julie (43)
  Betty (73)
  Joseph (15)
  Ember (16)

SETTING: Park

PROPS: Park bench, backpack with lunch bag inside, hooded sweatshirt

JULIE approaches BETTY, who sits on a park bench.

JULIE: Excuse me. Is anyone sitting here?

BETTY: No. You may sit here.

JULIE: Thank you. It's a beautiful day to come to the park, isn't it?

BETTY: Yes, it's a beautiful day.

JULIE: *(Points.)* That's my daughter coming down that slide. Her name is Hannah. She's eight.

BETTY: She's a cute girl.

JULIE: Thank you. She has so much energy. I'm hoping she will burn off some of it here at the park.

BETTY: *(Looks at her watch.)* Do you know when the bus will be here?

JULIE: The bus?

BETTY: I think it's late. Don't you?

JULIE: I don't believe the bus stops here.

BETTY: It does. It must be late.

JULIE: Where are you planning to go?

BETTY: Home.

JULIE: Where's home?

BETTY: *(Points.)* That way. For some reason, I can't remember the name of my street. What is it? What is it? Oh, it'll come to me in a minute.

JULIE: I don't mean to disagree with you, but I don't think the bus stops here. Not here at this park bench.

BETTY: Yes, it does. This is the bus stop.

JULIE: *(Jumps up, shouting at her offstage daughter.)* Hannah Marie, sit down this very second! *(To BETTY.)* She's such a tomboy. *(To daughter.)* I said, sit down! You're going to tumble down that slide!

BETTY: I never had any children.

JULIE: *(Sits.)* No?

BETTY: No.

JULIE: I have three children, just like my sister does. Hannah's my baby. The surprise of our family. She has a brother who's fifteen. Joseph. And a sister who's sixteen. Ember. Just when you think you've about raised your family... here comes a surprise. *(Smiles.)* But she has been a delight. For all of us.

BETTY: I never was the mother type. Wouldn't have known what to do with kids. In my opinion, they are... what's that word? Bothersome. Yes, bothersome.

JULIE: Yes, they can be at times. And yet, until you have a child of your own, you can't quite understand what it's like. The love you feel for a child is impossible to explain. There are just no words to describe it.

BETTY: *(Looks at her watch.)* I wish the bus would hurry up. It's late. But what can I do but wait?

JULIE: *(Jumps up.)* Hannah Marie! Sit down! Now! *(To BETTY.)* I swear she's going to really hurt herself one of these days. I just know it. *(Sits down and takes a lunch bag from her backpack. Opens it.)* Are you hungry? I brought an extra sandwich. Would you like one?

BETTY: Oh, no. Thank you, though. I ate earlier.

JULIE: Oh? What did you have?

BETTY: I had... well, I don't quite remember. I'm sure it'll come to me in a minute.

JULIE: Are you sure? I have a ham and swiss sandwich. With extra mayo just the way you—I mean, just the way I like to make it.

BETTY: Well, I guess I am a bit hungry.

JULIE: Here. Take this. I'm happy to share with you.

BETTY: *(Takes the sandwich.)* Thank you.

JULIE: My mother loved ham and swiss sandwiches. She made me a believer.

BETTY: *(Takes a bite.)* I do too. This is really good.

JULIE: On white bread. That's the only bread she would eat. I think it has zero nutritional value. But that's what she liked.

BETTY: Is your mother still around?

JULIE: She is, but... she's not well.

BETTY: I'm sorry to hear that.

JULIE: Thank you. It's hard at times.

BETTY: I've been staying with my daughter at her house. But I've been there too long. And today I decided that I want to go home. So I just woke up, got dressed, and walked out the door. It's time for me to go home. I need to plant some geraniums in the yard. I like the red ones. So bright and colorful. And I'm sure the weeds have just about taken over the flowerbed. I also need to trim the rosebushes. I have six bushes in my front yard. They are so beautiful when they bloom in the spring. I always cut a few to bring into the house. Don't you love roses?

JULIE: Yes. It sounds like you have a green thumb.

BETTY: Yes, I guess I do. I like to be outside. And I love flowers. My mother did too. And her name was Rose. Isn't that perfect? *(JULIE nods and smiles.)* Last year I planted... what are they called? You know, those little colorful flowers that tend to come back every spring?

JULIE: Moss rose?

BETTY: Yes! That's it. I do hope they come back this year. They're supposed to. Yes, I've been gone too long. Much too long.

JULIE: I'm sure your plants are doing quite well.

BETTY: Where is that bus? I need to get home.

JULIE: *(Stands.)* Hannah Marie! *(To BETTY.)* Excuse me for a moment. *(Looks OFF and motions someone to come over,* *then EXITS. JOSEPH ENTERS. He wears a hoodie with the hood up. He sits down next to BETTY.)*

JOSEPH: Hi.

BETTY: Hi. I don't mean to be rude, but someone is already sitting there.

JOSEPH: Oh. Well, I'll move when that person comes back.

BETTY: Maybe you should go stand over there. By that tree. I don't trust you.

JOSEPH: It'll be okay. I promise to move when your friend returns.

BETTY: *(Scoots away from him.)* She'll be right back. She's just checking on her daughter who's on the swing.

JOSEPH: That's my mom. She's checking on my little sister.

BETTY: *(Confused.)* Aren't you here waiting for the bus?

JOSEPH: No. I'm here with my mom.

BETTY: *(Stands.)* It's getting late.

JOSEPH: *(Stands.)* Where are you going?

BETTY: I'm going home.

JOSEPH: Where's home?

BETTY: *(Points.)* That way. I think. I was... uh... waiting for the bus.

JOSEPH: The bus doesn't come here. This is a park bench. You're at the park.

BETTY: *(Looks around, confused.)* No. This is the bus stop. *(Looks at watch.)* Why is it so late?

JOSEPH: The bus doesn't come to the park. See. Look around. See my little sister over there on that slide? This is the park.

BETTY: *(Confused.)* No... *(Sits back down.)* This is the bus stop. Right here. I've been staying at my daughter's house. She invited me to visit, but I've stayed too long and now I want to go home.

JOSEPH: Grandma, it's me, Joseph.

BETTY: Why did you call me Grandma?

JOSEPH: Look. It's me. Joseph. *(Nudges her.)* You know, your favorite grandson.

BETTY: *(Startled.)* Don't touch me. I don't know you.

JOSEPH: Yes, you do. You always say we're practically two peas in a pod. We both like sweets. And sometimes we sneak into the kitchen to share that last piece of cake. Or grab a handful of cookies. We've been doing that since I was old enough to walk. Remember? And you'd always say, "Don't tell your mom." And I'd say, "Never!" I never did tell her it was us. Even that time we ate the last half of her birthday cake. We were so bad, weren't we? Remember, Grandma? Remember?

BETTY: Stop it! I don't know you! You need to leave. This seat is taken.

JOSEPH: But, Grandma, it's me! Joseph.

BETTY: I will call the police if you don't leave. I don't know you.

JOSEPH: Yes, you do. Just look at me. Look into my eyes.

BETTY: *(Screams.)* Help! Someone help me!

JOSEPH: *(Stands.)* Okay, okay! I'm sorry. I'm moving over here. See? *(EMBER ENTERS.)*

EMBER: Joseph, what are you doing?

JOSEPH: I was trying to help.

BETTY: This hoodlum scares me!

EMBER: I'm so sorry. *(To JOSEPH. Whispers.)* Look what you've done. You've upset her.

JOSEPH: I'm sorry. I didn't mean to. I just thought—

EMBER: We've just got to accept that she's...

JOSEPH: I know. You stay with her. I'll go help Mom with Hannah.

BETTY: *(Points her finger at JOSEPH.)* Go. Leave me alone. I don't know you, and I don't want you here.

JOSEPH: I'm sorry. *(Steps towards her.)* I was just trying to help.

BETTY: *(Yells.)* Help! *(To EMBER.)* Please help me!

EMBER: Joseph!

JOSEPH: I'm going, I'm going. Sorry.

BETTY: *(To EMBER.)* Oh, thank you. Thank you. He scared me.

EMBER: I'm so glad I could help. May I sit here?

BETTY: This seat is taken. But I don't remember who it's for.

EMBER: When the person comes back I promise to move. Okay? Please?

BETTY: If you promise to move when they come back.

EMBER: *(Sits.)* I promise.

BETTY: That boy scared me. Did he scare you?

EMBER: No, not really. You're safe. I promise.

BETTY: I hope so. *(Pause.)* It's a pretty day to plant flowers. Don't you think?

EMBER: I do. What's your favorite kind of flower?

BETTY: Roses.

EMBER: I love roses. What's your favorite color?

BETTY: Red. Red roses. You know what they mean, don't you?

EMBER: Of course. They represent love. *(Puts arm around her.)* I love you.

BETTY: *(Scoots over a bit and EMBER drops her arm.)* I have red roses at my house. That's where I'm going today. Home. I want to plant them. *(Looks at her watch.)* I wish the bus would hurry up.

EMBER: Did you meet my mom? That's her over there with my sister, Hannah.

BETTY: I think I met her. She's nice. She was sitting here with me.

EMBER: Yes, she is nice. And since your bus is taking forever to get here, perhaps we could give you a ride home.

BETTY: Thank you, but I don't take rides from strangers.

EMBER: But you know us.

BETTY: No.

EMBER: You met my mom.

BETTY: *(Stares. Pause.)* I think I know her. But I forgot what her name is. Do you know what her name is?

EMBER: It's Julie.

BETTY: Julie. That's a pretty name.

EMBER: And I'm Ember.

BETTY: Ember. That's an odd name.

EMBER: *(Small laugh.)* I hear that sometimes. I'm sure my mom would be happy to give you a ride home. You don't want to keep waiting for the bus to show up, do you?

BETTY: No. I am tired of waiting. And I do have flowers to plant.

EMBER: *(Looks off and gives a thumbs up to her mom.)* Mom will be happy to give you a ride home. Then you can plant your flowers.

BETTY: *(Stands.)* And check on my roses. They need to be pruned. Do you want to help me?

EMBER: I'd love to help you.

JULIE: *(ENTERS. To EMBER.)* Joseph and Hannah are walking home. I think they have plans to stop and get ice cream.

EMBER: Mom, can you give this nice woman a ride home?

BETTY: How do you do? My name is Betty.

JULIE: Hello, Betty. I'm Julie.

BETTY: Hello, Julie.

EMBER: Nice to meet you, Betty.

BETTY: *(Looks at EMBER.)* What did you say your name was?

EMBER: Ember.

BETTY: Oh, right. The strange name. *(Looks at JULIE.)* Ember is going to help me prune my rose bushes.

JULIE: Oh, that's nice. So, are we all ready to go?

EMBER: Ready.

BETTY: Ready.

JULIE: *(Takes BETTY'S arm.)* Come on, Mom. Let's go home.

BETTY: I'm Betty. My name is Betty.

JULIE: *(Nods.)* Come on, Betty. Let's all go home.

WILDFLOWERS

SYNOPSIS: A woman tells the man she had a one-night stand with three months earlier that she is pregnant.

CAST: 1M, 1F, plus 1F walk-on
  Paul (28)
  Mia (25)
  Kendra (27)

SETTING: Doorway of an apartment
PROPS: None

MIA knocks on the door of PAUL'S apartment, and PAUL ENTERS to answer it.

MIA: Surprise!

PAUL: Mia! What are you doing here? How did you find me? How did you find my apartment? I never told you where I lived.

MIA: You didn't. And it wasn't easy to find you, but I'm glad I did! Did you change your phone number? I've been trying to call you, and I even left messages. I also sent you some texts. Didn't you get them?

PAUL: No, I... uh... How did you find my apartment?

MIA: Aren't you glad to see me?

PAUL: Yes, but... I'm surprised to see you. It's been what? About three months now? Uh... how are you?

MIA: I'm good. Really good. *(Hugs him awkwardly.)* Oh, Paul, it's so great to see you! One crazy weekend together at Coral Beach Resort, and then you were gone. I had to find you. You have no idea how much I've thought about you.

PAUL: I didn't think I'd ever see you again.

MIA: I've been trying to call you.

PAUL: I've been... you know... busy.

MIA: Well, that doesn't matter now. We can just pick up where we left off.

PAUL: Where we left off? Mia, we barely know each other.

MIA: Sure we know each other! We spent an entire weekend together. Talking, laughing, and snuggling. Getting to know each other. Oh! Remember the wildflowers that you picked for me at Coral Beach? I still have them. I pressed them into my *Potter's Bible.*

PAUL: Your what?

MIA: My *Potter's Bible.* It's a reference book for pottery lovers. Remember, I told you I make pottery?

PAUL: Sorry, I don't really... remember.

MIA: Anyway, I kept the flowers that you picked for me. Pressed them into the book for safekeeping so they'll last forever.

PAUL: Why?

MIA: Why? Because it was so romantic! Remember how you picked one flower of each color and then handed me that little bouquet? It was so sweet. I loved it. Oh, Paul, it's so wonderful to see you again.

PAUL: How did you find me?

MIA: I went online. I've been desperately looking for you.

PAUL: Desperately? Why? It was just one weekend.

MIA: I have so much to tell you!

PAUL: Really... we hardly know each other. That weekend was special, and I... I had a great time, but... you know, there was a lot going on with me then.

MIA: I know. You had just been dumped by your girlfriend. But you said it was the best thing that ever happened to you. "Good riddance" is what you said about her.

PAUL: Did I say that?

MIA: Yes. You said you were glad that she ended it, so you didn't have to. Remember? And it was because of all of that, that we met. You were all depressed sitting in that coffee shop by yourself. You looked so adorable, yet sad. And do you remember what I asked you?

PAUL: Not really.

MIA: Oh, come on! You remember. I asked you if you needed a smile.

PAUL: Oh, yeah.

MIA: And you shrugged.

PAUL: I remember.

MIA: So, I gave you a smile. You looked so sad, and I wanted to cheer you up.

PAUL: That's when you sat down at my table.

MIA: That's right. You gave me this painful look, and I gave you a smile. *(Smiles.)* Then you smiled back at me.

PAUL: I remember.

MIA: Then we ended up drinking coffee and talking for what seemed like hours. And then...

PAUL: A long walk up to Coral Beach Point.

MIA: I remember you saying that I had come along at just the right time and saved you.

PAUL: I was upset about Kendra—our fight and the breakup.

MIA: You snapped out of it pretty quickly though. After awhile, you said you were happy that she was out of your life. And then you picked me that purple flower and tucked it behind my ear.

PAUL: Uh, yeah. I do remember that.

MIA: Then you picked an orange flower, then a yellow one, a white one, another purple one and held them out to me. A perfect bouquet of wildflowers.

PAUL: I'm glad you liked them.

MIA: Oh, I loved them!

PAUL: So, why are you here?

MIA: Why? Because we had the most incredible weekend ever, and I wanted to see you again. Why did it have to end so suddenly? Did you say you changed your phone number?

PAUL: No, I—

MIA: You probably had to change it because your crazy ex-girlfriend was calling you all the time.

PAUL: No. We... uh... we worked it out.

MIA: What?

PAUL: Kendra and I worked it out. We're back together. It was just a stupid fight.

MIA: But... but you said it was over. You said, "Good riddance."

PAUL: I know. I was upset. At the time I thought it was over. But when I got home, Kendra explained how she was questioning everything in her life, including me. And to make matters worse, I had stopped making her a priority, and she felt we had lost our connection. That we'd become stagnant. It was a really good heart-to-heart.

MIA: Heart-to-heart?

PAUL: Yeah, a big one. Throw it all out there and find a solution. Fortunately, we were able to mend the broken areas of our relationship. We're better than ever now.

MIA: But you and I... we... we had an amazing weekend together.

PAUL: Yeah, and it was great. I'm sorry I let you think it was anything more than it was. You know, led you on.

MIA: Led me on?

PAUL: Made you think I cared for you.

MIA: You did make me think you cared for me.

PAUL: Mia, it was just one weekend.

MIA: Just one weekend? Don't you remember what you told me?

PAUL: No. Not really.

MIA: You said it was as if fireworks erupted when you met me. That our souls had connected in an explosive way, like nothing you had ever experienced before.

PAUL: Did I say that?

MIA: Yes.

PAUL: We needed each other for a night.

MIA: For a night? You mean, like a one-night stand?

PAUL: It happens. People get swept up in their emotions and lean on each other. Maybe it's because they're feeling lonely or running from some sort of pain or just need to feel another's touch. Mia, it was what we both needed at the time.

MIA: But I thought... I thought it meant something to you.

PAUL: You knew my heart was broken.

MIA: Yes, but you seemed to recover pretty quickly.

PAUL: I was tired of feeling sad. You helped me forget about it for a while. But you had to have known my heart was still with Kendra.

MIA: So you lied?

PAUL: I was trying to convince myself that I could move on.

MIA: By using me?

PAUL: It wasn't like that. Besides, haven't you ever hooked up with someone just for the fun of it?

MIA: No. Like I said, I thought I meant something to you. What about my feelings?

PAUL: What can I say? I'm sorry.

MIA: Well, I have something to say.

PAUL: What? You hate me? If it makes you feel better to say it, then say it. Is that it? You hate me.

MIA: *(Pause.)* I'm pregnant.

PAUL: *(Steps back.)* No, you're not. You couldn't be.

MIA: You think I'm lying?

PAUL: Maybe. Yes! You're lying, aren't you?

MIA: No.

PAUL: You can't be pregnant! You're just... just feeling jilted. I'm sorry to break it to you, but that was just a night to forget our troubles. A night of fun. A night of comfort. And that night... that night is over.

MIA: And here I thought you'd be happy to see me.

PAUL: I still can't believe you tracked me down to my apartment. I mean, who does that? Who tracks down a guy they had a one-night stand with except for some crazy lunatic?

MIA: Oh, so now I'm a crazy lunatic?

PAUL: Is this fun for you? What are you doing? Go find someone else to lie to and screw around with.

MIA: I can't believe you just said that to me.

PAUL: Look, I'm happy. Kendra and I are back together, and we're happy! It was just a one-night stand, okay? You've got to accept that. I'm sorry you thought we meant more to each other, but we don't. Sometimes things just happen. But I don't need you to be causing me and Kendra problems. *(Looks at his watch.)* In fact, she's going to be here in a few minutes. So if you don't mind, could you just, you know... leave? I don't want you here when she gets here.

MIA: I'm sorry I ever met you. And I thought you'd be happy to see me.

PAUL: Happy?

MIA: And to think I convinced myself you'd lost my phone number.

PAUL: I didn't.

MIA: Or you'd changed your phone number because of your crazy ex-girlfriend.

PAUL: I didn't.

MIA: And so it appears that I'm the crazy ex now.

PAUL: I didn't say that.

MIA: I did. Wow. Just wow. I get it now. *(Shakes head.)* How could I have been so stupid?

PAUL: Can we just pretend this never happened?

MIA: What about all those things you said? Where had I been all your life? How easy it was for you to get lost in my eyes. How you could fall in love with me. And did I believe at love at first sight?

PAUL: I'm sorry.

MIA: Why did you say all those things to me?

PAUL: I don't know. I guess it was because I was hurt, and I know girls like to hear that stuff.

MIA: So you just said it so we could hook up for a one-night stand?

PAUL: I wanted comfort. Distraction. You were doing the same thing.

MIA: No, I wasn't. I thought it was the beginning of a relationship that would blossom into something beautiful and magical. And maybe... just maybe... it really was love at first sight.

PAUL: You don't really believe in that, do you?

MIA: No. Not anymore.

PAUL: *(Looks at his watch.)* You need to go.

MIA: Did you even hear what I said?

PAUL: Sure, sure. You thought we had something special, and it was... you know... a mistake. I'm sorry. So what do we do now? We move on. That's what we do.

MIA: *(Steps back from him.)* Didn't you hear me? I'm pregnant.

PAUL: No, you're not. You can't be.

MIA: Oh, yes I am.

PAUL: No. I don't accept this. I think you're lying. You're desperate and lonely. *(Wags his finger in her face.)* But this isn't going to work on me.

MIA: Oh, so you prefer that I take it back? Pretend I never said it? Pretend we never met?

PAUL: Yes. Yes to all of that.

MIA: I see. So as you move on with Kendra, you don't want to be burdened with your child by a person who meant nothing to you other than a one-night stand.

PAUL: Well, yeah.

MIA: So when you walk through a mall or an amusement park and you see a cute kid, you won't wonder if that child is yours? Or what your child looks like? Or if it was a boy or a girl? And you're okay with this? Of me walking away and you never knowing?

PAUL: Sorry, but yeah. It's okay with me.

MIA: All right, then.

PAUL: That's it?

MIA: For now.

PAUL: What do you mean, "For now"?

MIA: I need to figure all this out. Alone.

PAUL: Like what? What do you have to figure out?

MIA: Do I walk away and do this by myself, or dig my heels in and force a practical stranger into my life for a child he doesn't want? Forcing you to pay child support and dealing with possible visitation. Seeing you at birthdays, holidays, and other awkward moments. Together, yet always apart.

PAUL: Look, I'm sorry, but I'm not good father material. You're better off doing this alone. *(Looks at his watch.)* Okay? Are we good here?

MIA: I'll let you know.

PAUL: Wait! I can't have this hanging over my head. What are you going to do?

MIA: What am I going to do? Well, first, I'm going to throw away those wildflowers.

PAUL: Wildflowers?

MIA: The ones I pressed in my book to save forever. *(Touches her belly.)* But then again, maybe I won't. Maybe I'll keep them.

PAUL: I need to know. What are you going to do? Tell me!

MIA: Don't worry. The flowers are going in the trash. And you and I… goodbye. *(Turns and EXITS. As she leaves, KENDRA ENTERS and gives PAUL a quick kiss hello.)*

KENDRA: Who was that?

PAUL: Uh… nobody.

ON THE COUNT OF THREE

SYNOPSIS: A young man feels responsible for his fiancée's tragic car accident that has left her in a coma.

CAST: 2M, 1F
    Tim (mid-20s)
    Nathan (20)
    Claire (20)

SETTING: Outside a hospital room
PROPS: None

Friends TIM and NATHAN stand outside CLAIRE'S hospital room, where she has been in a coma for a month after a car accident. We only see CLAIRE through NATHAN'S imagination.

TIM: Are you going in?

NATHAN: In a minute.

TIM: What are you waiting for?

NATHAN: *(Takes a deep breath.)* I just need a minute.

TIM: Come on. I'll go in with you.

NATHAN: You go ahead.

TIM: Nate, what's wrong?

NATHAN: Seriously? You're asking me that?

TIM: Come on. Claire needs you.

NATHAN: Needs me, Tim? She doesn't even know I'm here.

TIM: I don't believe that's true. Studies have shown—

NATHAN: Stop. Don't tell me about studies. There's no response. Nothing. As time goes on, things are looking worse. All the doctors are saying that. The only thing left to hope for is a miracle.

TIM: If anyone can pull my sister out of this coma, it's you. You guys love each other so much.

NATHAN: Pull her out? Me? Sure. Sure, I can. All I can think about is that night at Nick's. She wanted to leave, but I was too busy playing video games to listen to her.

TIM: It was her decision to leave without you.

NATHAN: But who can blame her? I was hanging out with the guys, completely ignoring her.

TIM: The accident wasn't your fault.

NATHAN: Not my fault? Of course it was my fault! I'm supposed to take care of her. What kind of fiancé tosses the car keys to his girlfriend and tells her she's on her own? I was too caught up in that stupid video game.

TIM: Listen to me. It was an accident.

NATHAN: Tim, are you listening to me? Claire's accident was my fault. It was because of my selfishness. Everyone knows it. So why don't you admit it too? Go ahead.

TIM: Everyone knows you loved her.

NATHAN: Loved? You make it sound like she's already gone. Well, I guess in one sense she is.

TIM: Everyone knows you would never do anything, ever, to hurt her.

NATHAN: No, but if I had paid attention to her and taken her home when she wanted to leave, this accident never would have happened.

TIM: You don't know that. The roads were icy that night. Maybe you'd both be fighting for your lives right now.

NATHAN: No, because I would have known not to take the highway in that weather. The overpasses are always the first to freeze up, and when you're going that fast—

TIM: You can't know for sure that you would've avoided an accident.

NATHAN: Yes, I would have! I would've taken Rancher's County Road. It's a lot safer. I didn't even think to tell Claire that when she left.

TIM: Come on. Let's go in and see how she's doing today. I thought yesterday she had a bit more color in her face.

NATHAN: *(Shakes his head.)* No, she's the same.

TIM: You know, I've heard that you should talk to people who are in a coma as if they can hear you.

NATHAN: She can't hear me.

TIM: Nate...

NATHAN: What?

TIM: Be positive. Give her a reason to wake up.

NATHAN: I've begged her to wake up!

TIM: Then tell her it's okay to take her time. Wait until she's ready. Until her body is strong enough. Just talk to her.

NATHAN: It's been a month. A month!

TIM: You can't give up.

NATHAN: I'm here, aren't I?

TIM: *(Frustrated.)* Well, even if you won't, I'm going in. *(EXITS as CLAIRE ENTERS and stands a few steps behind NATHAN, to one side.)*

CLAIRE: Nathan, are you giving up on me?

NATHAN: No.

CLAIRE: I wouldn't give up on you.

NATHAN: I'm here, aren't I?

CLAIRE: But where's your sweet smile? I've missed that smile.

NATHAN: I can't...

CLAIRE: I don't like seeing you sad.

NATHAN: I can't stand seeing you like this, all hooked up to tubes and stuff. I hate it.

CLAIRE: I'm not dead.

NATHAN: I know that, Claire!

CLAIRE: Remember last month when we went to the playground and acted like a couple of silly kids? I loved that swirly blue slide. *(Holds her hands up in the air.)* Wheee!

NATHAN: *(Small smile.)* You were so cute.

CLAIRE: I want to go down that blue slide again. Come with me! Let's go down together!

NATHAN: *(Remembering.)* Race you!

CLAIRE: Hey! Wait for me! Don't go down without me!

NATHAN: I don't want to do anything without you.

CLAIRE: I love doing everything together too.

NATHAN: Yes.

CLAIRE: Nathan?

NATHAN: Yeah?

CLAIRE: How long do you want to be with me?

NATHAN: Forever and ever.

CLAIRE: Are you just saying that? Tell me the truth. How long? How long will you love me?

NATHAN: *(Smiles. This is clearly a game they play.)* You tell me. How long will you love me?

CLAIRE: No. You tell me first.

NATHAN: No. You.

CLAIRE: No. You. *(They share a laugh.)*

NATHAN: Okay, on the count of three, we'll say our answer at the same time.

CLAIRE: All right.

NATHAN: One... two... three... *(After a pause.)* You didn't say anything.

CLAIRE: Okay, this time we'll really do it. On the count of three...

NATHAN: One... two... three...

NATHAN/CLAIRE: Forever.

CLAIRE: I love you.

NATHAN: I love you too.

CLAIRE: Do you miss me?

NATHAN: Intensely. I feel as if I can't breathe. Yesterday, I went to the park and sat at the top of the blue slide. I pretended that you were in front of me and I was holding you tight. But in reality, I went down the slide alone.

CLAIRE: We'll go back.

NATHAN: When?

CLAIRE: I'm not sure.

NATHAN: When, Claire? When?

CLAIRE: I'll always be a good memory.

NATHAN: Stop! Don't say that!

CLAIRE: Will you always think about me when you look at that slide?

NATHAN: Always.

CLAIRE: Maybe one day you'll have a little girl and you can take her to that park. And you can tell her about us. About all the fun that we had. But even if you don't want to tell her about me, you have to promise that you'll always remember me.

NATHAN: Stop it!

CLAIRE: I want to come back to you. I'm just not sure that I can.

NATHAN: If only you knew how much this was killing me on the inside.

CLAIRE: Let's play a game. On the count of three, we'll say the first thing that pops into our heads.

NATHAN: No, Claire.

CLAIRE: Come on, Nathan. This will be fun. Okay, so on the count of three say the first thing that pops into your head. No matter what. Stupid or silly. Maybe a confession or a secret or a fear.

NATHAN: Are you really going to make me do this?

CLAIRE: Yes. On the count of three. One... two... three... *(Silence.)*

NATHAN: You didn't say anything.

CLAIRE: Neither did you. Why do we always do this?

NATHAN: I don't know.

CLAIRE: Okay, this time really counts. Whatever you're thinking. On the count of three. One... two... three...

NATHAN: I want you to wake up. I want to hear your voice. I want us to hold hands again.

CLAIRE: I'm slipping away.

NATHAN: No! Don't do that! I need you!

CLAIRE: I need for you to be okay, Nathan.

NATHAN: I'm not okay, Claire. Do I look okay to you?

CLAIRE: No. Not really. Okay, on the count of three, we'll—

NATHAN: No! Stop it! *(Pause.)*

CLAIRE: Where's Blue Bear?

NATHAN: I brought him to your room.

CLAIRE: Where? I don't see him.

NATHAN: He's sitting on the windowsill.

CLAIRE: *(Delighted.)* Oh! There he is! I love that bear!

NATHAN: I know. That's why I brought him to you.

CLAIRE: You gave me Blue Bear on our three-month anniversary. I love him!

NATHAN: I know you do.

CLAIRE: I love you too.

NATHAN: *(About to break down.)* Oh, Claire...

CLAIRE: Please don't cry. It'll be okay. We had something special. Not everyone gets to experience a love like ours. Five magical years. Full of laughter. *(Suddenly laughs.)* Remember the time we made macaroni pizza? It was terrible! Whose idea was that anyways?

NATHAN: Mine.

CLAIRE: It tasted awful.

NATHAN: No kidding.

CLAIRE: But it was so much fun! And remember that time we slept outside under the stars?

NATHAN: I loved that.

CLAIRE: And how we took all of our freshman college classes together because we couldn't stand to be apart?

NATHAN: I still can't stand to be apart from you now.

CLAIRE: And how we walked along the railroad track as if we'd follow it to the end? Do you think it ever ends?

NATHAN: I hope not.

CLAIRE: I don't think it ends either. I think it just winds back around to where it started.

NATHAN: Remember when I proposed?

CLAIRE: *(Gleams, holding up her hand.)* How could I forget? That was the happiest day of my life.

NATHAN: And we were planning to get married this summer.

CLAIRE: Yes, we were.

NATHAN: Is it still the plan?

CLAIRE: *(Looks at her ring.)* I love my ring. It's so beautiful.

NATHAN: Are we still going to get married this summer?

CLAIRE: *(Smiles brightly.)* Okay, on the count of three—

NATHAN: Tell me. I need to know.

CLAIRE: Are you ready? On the count of three. One... two... three... *(Silence.)*

NATHAN: Why do we always do this? Every time? We count, then neither one of us says anything.

CLAIRE: It's just what we do.

NATHAN: Okay, on the count of three, you tell me if we're getting married this summer. That you'll be okay.

CLAIRE: You have to say what you think too.

NATHAN: All right. I will. On the count of three. One... two... three... *(Silence.)* I knew you wouldn't say anything. *(EXITS to her hospital room.)*

CLAIRE: *(Steps forward.)* On the count of three. One... two... three... *(Pause. Smiles wistfully.)* No. But in our dreams, we will always be together. I tried to come back. I wanted to come back to you, Nathan. No one will ever love me like you loved me. But don't you see? It was all worth it. Every tender moment. Every sweet kiss. Every race to that blue slide. The happiest moments of my life were when I was with you. I'm sorry I can't come back. But we still have our memories. Those can never be erased. Okay, on the count of three... *(NATHAN ENTERS and stands behind CLAIRE.)* ...we'll tell each other if it was all worth it. One... two... three... *(Silence.)* Come on. Say it. You have to say it this time. Even knowing how it ends, was it all worth it?

NATHAN/CLAIRE: Yes.

THE BEST DAY OF MY LIFE

SYNOPSIS: A young woman opens up about a past suicide attempt with someone she has just met.

CAST: 1M, 1F
    Bryan (26)
    Emma (23)

SETTING: Outside patio of a coffee shop
PROPS: Patio table, two chairs, two disposable coffee cups, spiral notebook, pen

EMMA sits outside a coffee shop. She is staring down at a spiral notebook, tapping her pen against the paper. BRYAN ENTERS, carrying a cup of coffee. He scours the patio area for an empty table, then, not finding one, he approaches EMMA.

BRYAN: May I sit here?

EMMA: *(Looks up.)* Sure.

BRYAN: Thank you. *(Sits down.)* It's a lovely day for some coffee and fresh air, don't you think?

EMMA: It is. *(Looks down at the notebook, taps her pen a few times, then looks back at him.)* Hey, may I ask you a question?

BRYAN: *(Holds up his left hand, smiling at her.)* Single.

EMMA: Not that.

BRYAN: You?

EMMA: *(Holds up her left hand.)* Single.

BRYAN: *(Offers his hand.)* I'm Bryan.

EMMA: *(Shakes his hand.)* Hi, I'm Emma.

BRYAN: And your question is?

EMMA: My question is this. If you had to write about either the best day or the worst day of your life, which would you choose?

BRYAN: May I ask you a question?

EMMA: Yes.

BRYAN: Why would you want to write about either one?

EMMA: I have a writing assignment due tomorrow. It's for my creative writing class at Hill Junior College. The prompt is to write about either the best or the worst day of your life.

BRYAN: Then that's easy. The worst.

EMMA: Why not the best?

BRYAN: The worst will get you a better grade. And if you fluff it up a bit, your professor may feel sorry for you and give you extra points.

EMMA: The worst day of my life, huh?

BRYAN: *(Sips his coffee.)* That's what I'd do.

EMMA: *(Taps pen on paper.)* The worst day of my life...

BRYAN: Like I said, you can always fluff it up a bit.

EMMA: No fluffing needed.

BRYAN: Sounds bad.

EMMA: It was.

BRYAN: So when did this happen? The worst day of your life?

EMMA: Actually, one year ago today. Exactly.

BRYAN: Wow, one year ago today was the worst day of your life?

EMMA: Yeah, ironic, isn't it? Especially since I'm working on this assignment today.

BRYAN: Then it's clearly a sign.

EMMA: But... *(Pause.)* I'm not sure that I want to write about it, or share it with anyone. You know? Even my instructor.

BRYAN: Hey, why don't you tell me about it? I'll be the judge.

EMMA: I don't know. I don't... you know... know you.

BRYAN: That should make it easier.

EMMA: I don't know. Maybe. But you go first. What was the worst day of your life?

BRYAN: That's easy. It was when my parents told me they were getting a divorce. I was fourteen. Dad had fallen in love with his co-worker, and he was leaving Mom so he could be *(Air quotes.)* "happy once and for all."

EMMA: Is he happy now?

BRYAN: No. He's still searching for it, mainly through booze, fast cars, and traveling. So, my motto is this. Enjoy your life for what it is and embrace the important things.

EMMA: Which are?

BRYAN: You don't know?

EMMA: I'm asking you. What do you consider the important things in life?

BRYAN: The simple things. *(Picks up his coffee.)* Sipping coffee on a beautiful day...

EMMA: That is very simple.

BRYAN: Making friends. *(He smiles at her.)* Realizing that it's okay to be yourself even if no one else likes who you are. It's important to like yourself, you know?

EMMA: *(Shrugs.)* That's not always easy.

BRYAN: Don't you like yourself?

EMMA: I suppose. At least more than I did a year ago.

BRYAN: That's good. Sounds like you're headed in the right direction.

EMMA: You have no idea how far I've come.

BRYAN: That's true. But what I do know is that no matter what happens, we need to be able to laugh at ourselves.

EMMA: Laugh at ourselves? *(BRYAN takes off his loafers.)* What are you doing?

BRYAN: Showing you my toes. *(Puts his feet on the table.)*

EMMA: Yes, okay. You have them. But I don't think you should put your feet on the table. People sit here and well... it's not polite.

BRYAN: Emma, look at my toes.

EMMA: Uh... I have no choice but to look at them, Bryan. Especially since you've practically put them in my face.

BRYAN: Please, I'm making a point here. Just look at my toes.

EMMA: Okay, I'm looking at your toes! Believe me, I'm looking at them. In fact, I really have no choice in the matter, do I?

BRYAN: Do you see? My third toe is longer than my second toe.

EMMA: Okay. And your point is?

BRYAN: It looks dumb, doesn't it?

EMMA: I don't know. Maybe. If you say so.

BRYAN: Look closer.

EMMA: *(Leans in. After a pause.)* I guess you're right. I suppose it does look dumb.

BRYAN: *(Small laugh.)* Thank you.

EMMA: I'm not sure what we're talking about. Your toes? How are they supposed to encourage me to write about the worst day of my life?

BRYAN: My point is this. I used to fret about my toes. Hide them. Feel ashamed. Embarrassed. I hated my toes. My dad. My life...

EMMA: I can understand that.

BRYAN: But why did I hate my life?

EMMA: Because your dad left your mom and broke up your family?

BRYAN: Yes.

EMMA: And because you have ugly toes?

BRYAN: *(Small laugh.)* Thanks.

EMMA: But you know, you should put them down. You know... off the table.

BRYAN: *(Moves his feet off the table.)* Right. Sorry. My point is this. Just like my toes, and my dad, we have to look at the larger picture. Don't waste your energy fretting over the things we can't change. Frustration and anger will only drag you down.

EMMA: So did you forgive your dad?

BRYAN: I did. Though that doesn't mean I'm not still sad about the life that he chose. But I can't let his actions control my happiness.

EMMA: You have a good attitude.

BRYAN: I haven't always. It took a bit of growing up first. So back to your assignment.

EMMA: *(Looks back at the notebook and taps her pen.)* The worst day of my life.

BRYAN: We all have bad days, Emma. Then we move on. Right?

EMMA: We're supposed to.

BRYAN: Spill it.

EMMA: Excuse me?

BRYAN: You owe me.

EMMA: I owe you?

BRYAN: I spilled my guts to you. So now it's your turn.

EMMA: All right. Since we're practically strangers, and I'll probably never see you again, what does it hurt?

BRYAN: Exactly.

EMMA: A year ago today... on my birthday—

BRYAN: Wait! Today's your birthday?

EMMA: Yes.

BRYAN: Happy birthday!

EMMA: Thanks.

BRYAN: *(Starts to sing.)* "Happy birthday to you, Happy birthday—"

EMMA: *(Raises her hand.)* No. Don't. Please.

BRYAN: Okay, okay. So, what happened last year?

EMMA: What happened last year... Well, in all honesty, I spiraled down to the pits of hell.

BRYAN: Wow. That sounds dark.

EMMA: It was.

BRYAN: What happened?

EMMA: I tried to kill myself.

BRYAN: What?! Why?

EMMA: I'm not sure the details are important now.

BRYAN: That's what you're going to write about?

EMMA: If I choose to write about the worst day of my life, then yes.

BRYAN: Look, I'm sorry. You don't have to explain anything to me. Really.

EMMA: Do you want to hear about it or not?

BRYAN: *(Sympathetically, he leans in.)* Sure. Sure, I do.

EMMA: So, I was in love. Have you ever heard of unrequited love?

BRYAN: Sure. Been there.

EMMA: Really?

BRYAN: Really. Jennifer Rogers. Yep. Jennifer Rogers hated my guts. But I'll spare you the details.

EMMA: Well, mine was Jake Taylor. I guess I had an overactive imagination, because I imagined that he loved me as much as I loved him. Fantasies are great until reality steps in.

BRYAN: So, what happened?

EMMA: Before or after I tried to kill myself?

BRYAN: Uh… before.

EMMA: I messed up.

BRYAN: How?

EMMA: By believing it was real. By believing that all I had to do was proclaim my love to Jake and he would run into my arms.

BRYAN: You shared your feelings with him?

EMMA: Yes. That was my first mistake. Jake couldn't have been more surprised, and not in a good way. As the saying goes, he looked like a deer caught in headlights.

BRYAN: I'm sorry.

EMMA: I'd played the scene in my head at least a million times, and I knew exactly how it would go. I'd be leaning against his car after classes were over. I'd be wearing a pretty sundress. The warm breeze would be blowing my hair back. And when he saw me, he'd smile, knowing I was there waiting for him.

BRYAN: Sounds nice.

EMMA: It was a disaster.

BRYAN: I'm sorry, Emma.

EMMA: So, Jake showed up, and I rambled on like a crazy person. I told him I had feelings for him and had decided to take a chance. A chance to find out if he had the same feelings I did. I was glowing with confidence. I knew he'd say yes.

BRYAN: And?

EMMA: And he wasn't happy or even touched with my abrupt confession. He sure didn't run into my arms as I had imagined he would. No. He said he was sorry, but he didn't feel a connection between the two of us. But, of course we could still be friends. Friends. I was humiliated. I ran away crying.

BRYAN: Jerk.

EMMA: No, he wasn't a jerk. It was me. It was all me.

BRYAN: Unrequited love, all right.

EMMA: Yes. So one year ago today—on my birthday—I decided I didn't want to deal with the humiliation of that experience for one more minute. I was lonely, embarrassed, and ashamed. So I decided to end it.

BRYAN: That's when you attempted suicide?

EMMA: Yeah. *(Pause.)* Do you think I should say how I tried to do it?

BRYAN: I'm not sure that's important. What's important is that you survived.

EMMA: I cut my wrists. *(Shows him.)* See?

BRYAN: *(Looks at her wrists, then places his hands around them.)* That's in your past, Emma.

EMMA: Did you see that? I tried to kill myself?

BRYAN: *(Still holding her arms in his hands.)* I saw it.

EMMA: So are you sorry?

BRYAN: For what?

EMMA: Sorry that you chose to sit with me today. Bet you weren't expecting all this.

BRYAN: No. But actually... I'm glad.

EMMA: Glad?

BRYAN: Yes. You made it through last year, and you're a stronger person now.

EMMA: Yeah... I'm glad it didn't work.

BRYAN: Me too.

EMMA: I'm not the same person I was a year ago.

BRYAN: I can see that.

EMMA: But I don't like the memory of what I did. And I'm sorry it was on my birthday of all days. It's a memory that will resurface every year for the rest of my life.

BRYAN: Which means...

EMMA: What?

BRYAN: That you must create a wonderful new memory!

EMMA: How I can do that?

BRYAN: *(Takes a sip of coffee, then smiles at her.)* I'd say having coffee with me is a good start.

EMMA: *(Smiles.)* Could be.

BRYAN: *(Takes her notebook and pen and draws quickly.)* For starters, you have to be happy with a birthday wish from a complete stranger. How old are you today?

EMMA: Twenty-three.

BRYAN: *(Still drawing.)* That's a lot of candles.

EMMA: What are you doing?

BRYAN: *(Holds up a picture of a birthday cake.)* Don't stop me this time.

EMMA: Stop you from what?

BRYAN: *(Sings.)* "Happy birthday to you. Happy birthday to you…"

EMMA: *(Smiles and laughs a little.)* Thank you. That was sweet.

BRYAN: Oh, you haven't seen anything yet. They sell cupcakes here, and I'm going to buy you one. Plus a gift certificate to this place so you can get your next few cups of coffee on me. You'll never forget about me on your birthday after this, will you?

EMMA: No, but… why are you doing this? You don't even know me.

BRYAN: Maybe I'd like to get to know you. After all, you tolerated my toes.

EMMA: *(Laughs.)* Your toes? Wow, you're so romantic.

BRYAN: I try. And maybe, who knows… maybe I can give you something to write about.

EMMA: What?

BRYAN: The best day of your life, I hope.

EMMA: You know, that's a much better subject to write about. Give me that spiral. *(Writes.)* "The Best Day of My Life."

BRYAN: *(Slips his shoes back on and stands.)* I'll be right back. One cupcake and a gift card coming up. *(EXITS humming the birthday song.)*

EMMA: *(As she writes.)* "The best day of my life was when it was my birthday, and I met a stranger whose presence felt as if it was meant to be. Energetic. Mysterious. Comfortable. Meaningful. As if the day were a birthday gift worth waiting for."

NO REGRETS

SYNOPSIS: A young man meets his father for the first time.

CAST: 2M
    Henry (46)
    Alex (28)

SETTING: Coffee shop
PROPS: Table, two chairs, two cups

HENRY and ALEX, father and son, are meeting for the first time at a coffee shop. ALEX sits at a table sipping coffee, and there's another cup of coffee on the table. HENRY ENTERS and approaches ALEX. They look at each other for a moment.

HENRY: Alex? *(Offers his hand.)* Hi. How are you?

ALEX: *(Stands. Shakes HENRY'S hand.)* I'm good. Good.

HENRY: That's good.

ALEX: Thanks for doing this.

HENRY: Sure. Not a problem.

ALEX: Do you want to sit down? I already ordered coffee.

HENRY: *(Sits down.)* Thanks. *(Takes a sip of the coffee.)* It's good.

ALEX: I really appreciate you meeting me here. I know it must be awkward for you.

HENRY: It was a surprise when you contacted me. But I'm glad you did. I mean, how often do you get to meet your son for the first time?

ALEX: *(Small, nervous laugh.)* Not too often, I imagine.

HENRY: So, how did you get my address?

ALEX: Well, I spent the last few years searching for you online. I contacted several people by the name of Henry Farquhar and then, well, you responded.

HENRY: When I saw Linda's name... your mom...

ALEX: I didn't have much to go on. Just a name. *(Small laugh.)* At least it's not too common a last name.

HENRY: Yeah. Since I moved from Gatesville, it had to make your search even more difficult.

ALEX: It did. I didn't have anything to go on. No relatives. Nothing. Like I said, just a name.

HENRY: I have a brother somewhere up north, but I haven't talked to him in years. You could say I'm pretty much a loner.

ALEX: I'm kind of that way too.

HENRY: Really?

ALEX: Yeah. I like my time alone.

HENRY: Me too.

ALEX: Mom said you knew about me.

HENRY: Yep! As they say, a bun in the oven!

ALEX: Huh?

HENRY: Your mom told me she was pregnant.

ALEX: Uh... yeah.

HENRY: Let me tell you, it was a surprise.

ALEX: Mom said that you weren't ready. For a kid, that is.

HENRY: Yeah, that's true.

ALEX: She explained it all to me. As much as she could. I mean, it wasn't as if you two were in love. At least that's what she said.

HENRY: No. We knew each other, but it was just one night...

ALEX: She told me. She knew your name from school, and that was about it.

HENRY: And you turned out just fine, didn't you?

ALEX: Somewhat.

HENRY: Somewhat? You're a handsome young man. I bet you're smart too, aren't you? Did you go to college?

ALEX: Law school.

HENRY: Law school? Well, what do you know? My kid's a lawyer. *(Chuckles.)* Hey, can I get some free legal advice?

ALEX: Yeah, uh, sure.

HENRY: No. Seriously, I may need some advice. Got myself into a little trouble a few months ago. I told them it wasn't mine, but they didn't believe me. I think someone set me up. I don't do drugs.

ALEX: Drug charges?

HENRY: Yeah. I'm out on bond. Someone framed me. I spent some time in jail, and let me tell you, that was no picnic. Anyway, I'm trying to get the charges dropped. The attorney who's assigned to my case doesn't believe me when I tell him that I was set up. I tried telling the cops the stuff wasn't mine, but they didn't believe me either. *(Pause.)* So, lawyer-son-of-mine, maybe you can offer your dad a little free legal representation. You don't mind, do you?

ALEX: I have a question for you first.

HENRY: Shoot.

ALEX: Did you ever look for me?

HENRY: Did I ever look for you? Like search for your mom? Look on the Internet? Try to find out where you were?

ALEX: Yeah. Did you?

HENRY: I thought about it.

ALEX: So the answer is no?

HENRY: Hey, I thought you'd be better off imagining that you had a father somewhere out there who had it all together, because I sure didn't. I was far from having my life together. Guess I still am. But, anyway, you had the opportunity to think your daddy was some rich and famous person. Not some poor, ordinary guy, which is pretty much what I am.

ALEX: So you never tried?

HENRY: I tried to let you live your own life.

ALEX: Did you know where I was?

HENRY: Oh, I figured you were still in Gatesville. Didn't think your mom would ever let you get too far. But I had no way of knowing for sure.

ALEX: I got the impression you didn't know her very well.

HENRY: We went to the same school. We knew each other, but we weren't exactly friends.

ALEX: You were more than friends at one point.

HENRY: A mistake.

ALEX: Mistake?

HENRY: That night was a mistake. Yep. A big mistake.

ALEX: *(Stands. Offers hand.)* It was nice meeting you, Henry.

HENRY: That's it? I thought we'd get to know each other.

ALEX: You've had twenty-eight years to get to know me. I'm the one who went looking for you.

HENRY: Hey, I figured you'd come find me when you were ready to.

ALEX: I was hoping you'd come looking for me, but you didn't. You even said you knew I still lived in Gatesville.

HENRY: I said I figured you still lived in Gatesville. Wasn't a hundred percent sure. Besides, I was going through a lot. A couple of divorces. Three kids. Child support. Two jobs. Money has been a bit scarce for me. What if you just wanted to find me so I'd give you money? Like back child support or something.

ALEX: *(Sits back down.)* You have three other kids?

HENRY: Yeah. Kylee, James, and Branson. You know what that means, don't you?

ALEX: What?

HENRY: You've got two half-brothers and a half-sister. What do you think about that?

ALEX: Where do they live?

HENRY: Well, to tell you the truth, I'm not really sure. I divorced their mothers and, well, we lost touch. But if you wanted to meet your half-siblings, I could do some looking around and see if I can find them.

ALEX: I take it that you don't want to see them either.

HENRY: Alex, I don't mean to disappoint you, but I'm not exactly father material.

ALEX: How can you say that when you have four kids?

HENRY: Like I said earlier, I'm a bit of a loner. Hey, you said you were too.

ALEX: I only meant I enjoy having alone time. Not distancing myself from my family and avoiding all responsibility.

HENRY: I tried to be there for you kids, but—

ALEX: You never tried. Not for me.

HENRY: You know what I mean. But I'm the kind of person who needs his space. I need to move around. To experience life. Kids will pull you down, you know? Always needing something. Tie my shoe. Play ball with me. Help me do my homework. And money. Always needing money. Do I look like I have a lot of money? Son, I'm sorry, but—

ALEX: Don't call me that.

HENRY: What?

ALEX: Son. Don't call me that.

HENRY: Look, you got yourself through college without a dime from me. You should be very proud of yourself.

ALEX: My mom and grandparents helped put me through college. Plus, I worked two jobs.

HENRY: Well, there you go! You found the help that you needed. Couldn't find it with me. No-siree.

ALEX: Thanks for meeting me.

HENRY: Really? That's it?

ALEX: What else is there?

HENRY: Don't you want to know more about me? Your dad? Like what my favorite music is? What do you think it is?

ALEX: I don't know.

HENRY: Classic rock! Give me some Lynyrd Skynyrd and AC/DC! *(Sings.)* "I'm on a highway to..." Well, never mind. That's probably not your kind of music, is it? Just don't tell me you like that country stuff.

ALEX: I don't mind it. I like all kinds of music, and country music is one of them.

HENRY: So we have some differences here and there. That's to be expected, right? What else do you want to know? Oh! My talents. Just in case you take after me. I can play the harmonica. And quite well, I might add. Dang. I wish I had brought it with me. I'd play it for you. *(Mimics playing the harmonica.)* I bet you'd be impressed, son.

ALEX: I said, don't call me that.

HENRY: Why not? You are my son.

ALEX: Call me Alex. Please.

HENRY: Okay. Alex. *(Smiles.)* The gals always like it when I played the harmonica. You've gotta have a talent. At least one. And that is mine. *(Again mimics playing the harmonica.)* So, was there something else you wanted to know about your old man?

ALEX: No, I don't think so.

HENRY: Oh, come on! Wouldn't you like to know more about your pop here? Like, did I charm the girls? Well, of course I did. Or better yet, how did I charm the girls? Well, let me let you in on a little secret. It's called having suave. You can't really learn it, but hopefully you've inherited this smooth and sophisticated quality from your dad. If you have, then you're one lucky man. *(Does a little move.)* Yes, it's called having suave.

ALEX: I guess you threw that little act on my mother, huh?

HENRY: I did and she came a-runnin'.

ALEX: And then?

HENRY: And then? Well, I wasn't a one-woman man. You understand that, don't you? I had to share my charm with others. Spread myself around, you know?

ALEX: Women want to be loved. Not left.

HENRY: Well, I have no regrets.

ALEX: Yeah. Neither does my mom.

HENRY: Oh, really?

ALEX: Mom said I was the prize from a hard lesson learned.

HENRY: Sounds like something she would say. So tell me, did you get your dad's charming personality?

ALEX: No. I got my mother's sense of responsibility. Ethics. Hard-working attitude.

HENRY: I see. Well, you should hang around me sometime and get some pointers. Like tonight, I'm hitting Joe's Bar. Come with me and I'll show you how it's done. *(Nudges him.)* How to charm the ladies, that is. It's actually pretty simple. You just ignore them, but at the right moment, give them a little wink and soon they'll be all over you. How simple is that? So, are you up for a night out with me?

ALEX: No, I can't. I'm married. Lindsey and I have a three-year-old, and I spend my evenings with them.

HENRY: I'm a grandfather? *(Chuckles.)* Oh, don't tell me that! That makes me sound so old.

ALEX: You're not a grandfather. Or a father for that matter.

HENRY: Well, technically—

ALEX: Technicalities don't make you a parent. Being there, sacrificing, loving, leading them in the right direction, hurting when they hurt, being proud when they succeed... that's what makes you a parent.

HENRY: That's what I was saying. All that kind of stuff ties me down too much. Sure you don't want to hit the bar with me tonight? I'm sure what's her name... oh, Lindsey won't mind.

ALEX: I'm sure. I have everything I need at home with my wife and my son.

HENRY: So, you got any more questions for me?

ALEX: No, I think you answered all my questions. I'm ready to walk away and get on with my life now. With no regrets.

HENRY: *(Offers his hand.)* No regrets. *(They shake hands.)*

ALEX: Thanks again for meeting me.

HENRY: Yeah, see ya. *(ALEX EXITS.)* Nice meeting you, son. Yeah. Nice meeting you.

SWEET REVENGE

SYNOPSIS: Now a movie star, a young woman returns to her ten-year reunion from high school, where she was always shunned by the popular cliques.

CAST: 5F
> Marci (27 or 28)
> Jennifer (27 or 28)
> Whitney (27 or 28)
> Mischa (27 or 28)
> Lilly (27 or 28)

SETTING: Restroom by a hotel ballroom
PROPS: Counter, yearbooks, pen, purses with makeup and hair supplies

MARCI stands in the restroom of a hotel ballroom where her ten-year high school reunion is taking place. She stands at the counter and looks out over the audience as if staring at herself in a mirror. She touches up her makeup, then takes a deep breath.

MARCI: *(To herself.)* The day has finally arrived. I've waited ten years for this moment of sweet revenge. Soon, I will enter that ballroom and sashay past each and every one of them as their eyes are fixed on me. Me. They'll all be there because of me. In awe. Whispering, pointing, mesmerized. "Look, there she is. It's Marci Collins." Yes, it is me. Or is that I? Yes, it is I. This is my moment. As they move toward me, I won't even bother to look their way. Why should I? They never looked at me back then. Instead, I will dismiss them. No words needed. *(Waves her hand in the air.)* As if they're but a mere irritant. *(Waves her hand again.)* Goodbye. Goodbye.

JENNIFER: *(ENTERS, surprised to find MARCI.)* Marci. Is that you?

MARCI: Yes. It is I.

JENNIFER: I can't believe it. I can't believe you're here! Everyone is talking about you. We were all wondering if you would show up for the reunion. And here you are. In the bathroom of all places. *(Pauses as she stares.)* Wow. Marci Collins. Right here. So, how are you? Oh, wait. Do you think...? I mean, would you mind if I got your autograph? *(Searches for a pen in her purse.)* I know I have a pen somewhere.

MARCI: Sure.

JENNIFER: Here it is. *(Searches more.)* Paper. Paper. Oh, I know. You can write in my yearbook. I brought it so we could look back at all of our old pictures. Oh my God! Some of our hairstyles were so ridiculous. *(Opens the yearbook.)* Let me find your picture. Oh, here you are. Wow. You've changed so much! It's hard to believe that was actually you back then. Wow. *(Offers her the yearbook.)* Here. I'd love it if you could sign this.

MARCI: First time for everything. *(Signs the book.)*

JENNIFER: *(Staring.)* Wow. I know I keep saying that. But wow. You don't even look the same. Like, who would recognize you? No one.

MARCI: Let's look at your picture. *(Flips a few pages.)* Here you are. Hmmm... I don't believe you've changed at all, Jennifer. Same hairstyle, same look, same everything.

JENNIFER: You don't think I've changed?

MARCI: Not really.

JENNIFER: I still can't believe I'm standing here next to you. I mean, I know we went to school together, and we were friends back then, but—

MARCI: Friends? We weren't friends back then.

JENNIFER: Sure we were. I've told everyone at work how we were friends in high school.

MARCI: Friends? You and I?

JENNIFER: Of course! We had classes together, we ate in the same lunchroom, we passed each other in the halls every day.

MARCI: Yes. We passed each other in the halls every day, but you never spoke to me.

JENNIFER: Of course I did.

MARCI: No, you didn't. You never spoke to me.

JENNIFER: I know we didn't exactly run in the same circles, but we knew each other.

MARCI: That part is true. We did know each other.

JENNIFER: And now... look at you.

MARCI: *(Looks in the mirror.)* How do I look?

JENNIFER: You look amazing. Just like you do in all of your movies. I've seen all of them, you know.

MARCI: Have you?

JENNIFER: Oh, yes. My favorite is *The Lilac Room*. I love that movie. And your co-star, John Peters... oh my God, what a heartthrob. I can't believe you got to spend all that time with him. And kiss him. Ooohhh! If that were me, I'd have died right there. *(Looks back at the yearbook.)* And to think, this was you back in high school. Hardly anyone knew you. So I have to ask, how did you do this? *(Motions to MARCI.)* This. This major transformation. Now you're so beautiful and talented. And sought out by so many fans, including me. *(Holds up the yearbook.)* I mean, who knew back then that you'd become a famous movie star?

MARCI: I knew.

JENNIFER: You did? Really?

MARCI: Sure. I had a dream, and I pursued it. I love acting. Always have. And who was going to stop me? The snobs at Richardson High who never spoke to me?

JENNIFER: Wow. If only I'd known.

MARCI: What? What would you have done differently?

JENNIFER: *(Small laugh.)* I would've made sure we were best friends.

MARCI: Jennifer, you had the chance to be my friend in high school.

JENNIFER: I know, but you were—

MARCI: What?

JENNIFER: You know.

MARCI: What? *(After a pause.)* What was I in high school? Tell me.

JENNIFER: Well, not part of any group. Not part of mine, at least. You were a nobody back then. *(MARCI dismisses JENNFIER with a wave of her hand, as she had practiced.)*

Oh, you want me to go now? Uh... okay, whatever you want. See you out there. *(EXITS.)*

MARCI: *(Looks back in mirror.)* Well, I'm somebody now, aren't I? Jennifer, I was somebody back then too, but you didn't notice me without my fancy clothes, makeup, and attitude. Back then, you had those things, but now it's my turn. I worked hard to get my big break. A breakout movie, to be exact. And awards. Movie offers. Money. So you like me now? *(Looks in the mirror. Smiles.)* Marci Collins, you have arrived. *(WHITNEY and MISCHA ENTER.)*

WHITNEY: Oh my God, it's true. You're here!

MISCHA: We didn't think you'd show up.

WHITNEY: At least not without security.

MARCI: Didn't you see him? He's standing outside the door.

WHITNEY: *(Motions to the door.)* That's your bodyguard out there?

MARCI: Yes, my agent insisted I'd need one to keep all the photographers away.

MISCHA: We thought he was a hotel employee or somebody like that.

WHITNEY: But now that I think about it, he doesn't look like anyone who would just be working for the hotel.

MISCHA: You should see all the photographers in the ballroom! There must be a dozen of them!

WHITNEY: Everyone's been asking, will *the* Marci Collins attend our ten-year reunion?

MISCHA: And the answer is yes! You're here.

WHITNEY: *(To MISCHA.)* This is great.

MISCHA: I can't believe it. You look amazing, Marci. So different after ten years. Who would've known?

MARCI: If you had known, what would you have done differently?

MISCHA: You mean back in high school?

WHITNEY: I would have gotten to know you better, that's for sure.

MISCHA: Do you want to sit with us at our table tonight?

WHITNEY: Yes, please sit with us! *(To MISCHA.)* You know, we might get our pictures in the magazines too! *(As if reading a picture caption.)* "Marci Collins sits with good friends at her high school reunion."

MISCHA: Ooh! You're right!

WHITNEY: Photo ops! *(They both take a moment to check their makeup and hair in the mirror.)*

MARCI: Thank you for the invitation, but I won't be staying for long. Just long enough to make an entrance.

WHITNEY: Well, if you change your mind, we'd love to have you sit at our table.

MISCHA: Definitely.

MARCI: Really? You'd love to have me sit at your table?

MISCHA: Yes, of course.

WHITNEY: Absolutely.

MARCI: Not like back then, huh?

MISCHA: What?

MARCI: You never invited me—or allowed me—to sit at your table back in high school. I was beneath you. A nobody.

MISCHA: That's not true.

WHITNEY: Mischa is right. We never felt that way. And besides, who remembers all that silly high school stuff?

MARCI: I do. Actually, I remember all of it very well. Don't you?

MISCHA: Oh, come on, you were fabulous back then.

WHITNEY: Just as you are now.

MARCI: Really? You never spoke to me.

WHITNEY: Of course we did.

MISCHA: It's just you were... you know.

MARCI: What?

WHITNEY: Shy.

MISCHA: Whitney is right. You were shy. But we still liked you.

MARCI: No, you didn't. And no, I wasn't shy. I just didn't fit into your tight circle of friends. You all deemed me unacceptable for some unknown reason. I wanted to fit into your group. I tried, but no. The high and mighty who graced the halls of Richardson High determined my place on the bottom rung of the social ladder. And for some idiotic reason, I accepted it. You had that power, not just over me, but over others as well. You granted popularity or crushed spirits. I wonder how you got so much power? Who were you to say?

WHITNEY: *(Shrugs.)* I guess it was our time.

MISCHA: Our moment to shine.

WHITNEY: Now it's your turn to rise to the top.

MISCHA: Your turn to shine.

MARCI: So I guess your time has ended. *(Waves her hand dismissively. WHITNEY and MISCHA stare at her, confused. MARCI gestures again.)* Excuse me, everyone is awaiting my arrival.

WHITNEY: Uh, sure. We'll go tell everyone you're coming. *(EXITS with MISCHA.)*

MARCI: *(Looks at herself in the mirror.)* Like me now, do you? Well, I'm sorry to say the feeling is not mutual. Marci Collins, how does it feel to be on top? *(Smiles.)* Wonderful. Blissful. This revenge is even sweeter than I planned.

LILLY: *(ENTERS. Softly.)* Marci?

MARCI: Lilly?

LILLY: *(Smiles.)* You really are here.

MARCI: *(Smiles, more genuinely than we've seen before.)* You bet I am.

LILLY: That's what I heard. The whole room is buzzing. All of the photographers are looking for you. And here you are, hiding in the bathroom.

MARCI: I'm not hiding. Well, maybe I am.

LILLY: I heard Mischa and Whitney telling half the room that you were in here. I tried coming in, but your security guy stopped me. He said he wasn't letting anyone else come inside. There are at least twenty girls outside the door trying to get in.

MARCI: Then how did you get in?

LILLY: I told him the truth.

MARCI: The truth?

LILLY: I told him that I'd been your best friend in high school. He said, "Sure, sure. Everyone's claiming to have been Marci's best friend."

MARCI: Everyone's saying that? Figures.

LILLY: But then I showed him what you wrote in my yearbook. *(Opens the yearbook and reads aloud.)* "Lilly, I don't think I could have survived high school without you. You are my one and only true friend. And never forget the promise we made to each other. One day, one day very soon, we will show them all." *(Pause.)* You sure showed them. And those girls out there—Jennifer, Whitney, and Mischa—now they're bragging to all those photographers about talking to you.

MARCI: I know. It's sad, isn't it? They're so full of themselves, just like ten years ago. But now, I can dismiss them with a wave of my hand. I did that to all three of them just now. *(Laughs.)* You should have seen it!

LILLY: *(Not finding it humorous.)* Really? You did that?

MARCI: *(Laughs again.)* It was classic! I've been planning this revenge since graduation!

LILLY: *(Takes a step back.)* Gee, Marci...

MARCI: What? What's wrong?

LILLY: That's what they used to do to us.

MARCI: I know! Isn't it great?

LILLY: Great? Great that you've become like them? No, I don't think so. Are you going to dismiss me next?

MARCI: Oh, no! I would never do that. You're my friend. *(Pause.)* I'm sorry I didn't stay in touch with you.

LILLY: It's all right. *(Small laugh.)* Hey, you were busy becoming famous. One little commercial, then wham. You got a starring role in a major film and were an overnight sensation.

MARCI: It certainly changed everything.

LILLY: For better or worse.

MARCI: Huh? What do you mean by that?

LILLY: *(Hesitates.)* Well, don't take this wrong. I mean, I'm really happy for you and all. I know this is what you've always wanted and worked for, but it just seems like it's changed you.

MARCI: Of course it has! Just look at me! I'm beautiful now, and rich and famous too. I'm so popular, I can go to any party I want, any restaurant that others have to wait months to get a reservation. I'm living the life!

LILLY: But don't you see?

MARCI: See what?

LILLY: You've become just like them. Acting like everyone else is beneath you. That you're better than everyone else.

MARCI: Really? Is that what you think?

LILLY: Honestly? Yes. Just listen to yourself.

MARCI: *(Moment of realization.)* Oh my God. It's true, isn't it? Here I'm being mean and condescending to get my revenge. But all I've accomplished is becoming as awful now as they were then. We hated how they used to treat us, and now I'm acting the exact same way.

LILLY: You don't have to be like this, you know.

MARCI: Oh, you're right! I thought revenge would be so sweet, but it just turned me into the worst of them. And here I've been so self-absorbed, I haven't even asked about you. Did you become a nurse like you planned?

LILLY: No. I became a mother. Remember Paul Taylor? He and I married two years after graduating. I have two daughters.

MARCI: You're a mom?

LILLY: Yes. Hannah is six, and Grace is four.

MARCI: Oh, that's wonderful! I'd love to meet your daughters.

LILLY: They'd love to meet you too. But I must warn you that they are a bit, shall I say, energetic. They will force you to have a tea party followed by a pretend visit to the beauty shop. You might end up with twenty or so hair clips and bows in your hair.

MARCI: I'd love that! *(Laughs.)* Remember when we were practically that young how we used to put glitter in our hair?

LILLY: *(Laughs.)* Yes. I'm sure everyone was laughing at us, but we thought we looked marvelous!

MARCI: Didn't we?

LILLY: I think so. *(Flips hair.)* Fabulous!

MARCI: *(Flips hair.)* Yes, fabulous. Oh, Lilly... I'm sorry. Thank you for bringing me back to reality.

LILLY: It's nice to have you back. You were always my best friend, Marci.

MARCI: I've missed you. I haven't had a friend like you since high school. *(They hug.)*

LILLY: *(Gets serious.)* This is the day we always talked about. Like in the yearbook. "One day, we will show them all." And you did. The entire room out there is buzzing about you.

MARCI: *(Looks in the mirror.)* And I'm hiding in the bathroom.

LILLY: Take a deep breath. Then swing open that door and walk right out there. Hold your head up high as you enter that ballroom with pride. This is your moment. You deserve this.

MARCI: Do I? Do I really?

LILLY: Yes, of course you do.

MARCI: Or am I still being as cruel as they were in high school by walking out there and acting superior to them?

LILLY: The difference is that's not who you are. You can be at the top without looking down on others.

MARCI: We both endured the pain.

LILLY: Yes. Yes, we did. So do this for both of us.

MARCI: I will, but... will you walk out there with me?

LILLY: Me?

MARCI: Yes. After all, we were best friends. We were always there for each other, and I'd like that to stay the same.

LILLY: Are you sure?

MARCI: I've never been so positive about anything. I've missed you.

LILLY: I've missed you too. *(They hug again.)*

MARCI: Now, if only...

LILLY: Only what?

MARCI: If only we had some glitter for our hair for old time's sake.

LILLY: If only. *(Raises her hand above their heads as if sprinkling glitter.)* It's magical glitter just for us.

MARCI: Perfect.

LILLY: *(Squeezes her hand.)* Gather your thoughts. I'll be right outside the door when you're ready.

MARCI: Thank you, Lilly. Thank you. *(LILLY EXITS. MARCI looks in the mirror, then takes a deep breath.)* Yes, you have arrived. Nothing fake. Nothing imagined. This is your moment, Marci Collins. Your time to shine. *(Smiles at her reflection, then shoulders back, head tall, she EXITS.)*

BROTHERS

SYNOPSIS: A young man stands at the gravestone of his younger brother, who he accidentally killed eight years earlier.

CAST: 3M
    David (24)
    Groundskeeper (60s)
    Kyle (26)

SETTTING: Cemetery

PROPS: Gravestone (optional), trash bag, piece of trash

DAVID stands at the gravestone of his younger brother, Timmy. Today would have been his eighteenth birthday.

DAVID: *(To the gravestone.)* I'm sorry. Not that it helps anything. Or changes anything. I just want to say it again... and again and again. Not that you can hear me. But if you could... if you can... I'm sorry. *(Shakes his head.)*

GROUNDSKEEPER: *(ENTERS carrying a trash bag.)* You doing all right today, son?

DAVID: Yes, sir. And you?

GROUNDSKEEPER: Doing good. Doing good. Just trying to keep this place nice. The trash blows in from somewhere. I always wonder where it comes from. There's not any businesses close to this cemetery. And people don't come here to have a picnic or empty the trash out of their cars. *(Picks up a piece of trash.)* But it seems to grow like weeds. And don't get me started on the actual weeds, that's another story.

DAVID: You do a good job keeping the place nice.

GROUNDSKEEPER: Thank you. I've worked here for twelve years. I take pride in my work. I do it for them, you know. *(Gestures to the surrounding area, suggesting other gravestones.)* I feel like I know the people who are laid to rest here. Granted, I may only know their names, but I feel connected to them. And sometimes we have these conversations. Sure, one-sided. Or... I don't know... maybe not. *(Motions to the grave.)* Relative of yours?

DAVID: My little brother. He would've been eighteen today.

GROUNDSKEEPER: Timothy.

DAVID: Timmy.

GROUNDSKEEPER: Let's see... he was ten when he...

DAVID: Yeah, he was only ten years old when he died.

GROUNDSKEEPER: I'm sorry.

DAVID: Me too. I come out to visit him every year on his birthday.

GROUNDSKEEPER: That's nice.

DAVID: Not that he knows.

GROUNDSKEEPER: Who's to know for sure?

DAVID: Yeah. Who's to know?

GROUNDSKEEPER: Accident?

DAVID: Yeah.

GROUNDSKEEPER: Sorry to hear that. But you know, when it's your time, it's your time. I had a sister who died of SIDS when she was a baby. You know, when babies fall asleep and stop breathing? Horrible, horrible time for my parents. Things like that aren't supposed to happen. But they do. So I guess we all have our time. It's just hard for those left behind to understand.

DAVID: It wasn't his time.

GROUNDSKEEPER: That's when you have to dig deep and find your faith. Faith that you'll see each other again.

DAVID: You believe that?

GROUNDSKEEPER: 'Course I do. *(Waves his arm slowly across the cemetery.)* I even have faith I'll meet some of these souls one day. I feel like they're my friends, and we share things in common. For instance, Mr. Ernest Tiffertiller, born in 1925, who passed away in 2013, has heard all about my dear Bessie Mae, who was laid to rest a few years ago. Why? His wife was named Bessie too. We have that in common. And over there... *(Points.)* Mattie Crook's grass around her grave is always greener than everyone else's, so I figure she was a quite a gardener. *(Small laugh.)* I asked her what her secret was. And Reuben over there must've been a huge baseball fan since he has baseball symbols on his tombstone. So, sometimes I go over there and let him know what the latest scores are and who I think is headed for the World Series. Yeah, we talk. And I think we'll meet one day too. *(Gestures to the grave in front of them.)* I've also said a few words to Timmy.

DAVID: You have?

GROUNDSKEEPER: Sure, I have. I told Timmy that when I was his age, I liked to go fishing with my dad. Did he like to fish?

DAVID: He did.

GROUNDSKEEPER: See. I knew we had something in common.

DAVID: Thanks.

GROUNDSKEEPER: For what?

DAVID: For talking to Timmy.

GROUNDSKEEPER: No thanks necessary. Have a good day.

DAVID: Thank you. You too. *(GROUNDSKEEPER EXITS.)*

DAVID: *(To gravestone.)* I wish I knew you could hear me. If only... Do you know what I'd tell you? I'd tell you that I'd give my life to change what happened. Did you know that, Timmy? I would. I'd trade places with you in a heartbeat. Geez, you were a great kid. I know, I know. I picked on you all the time. But that's what big brothers do, right? Remember how I'd tease you about liking Kristi down the street? You'd deny it all day long, but I was right, wasn't I? You liked her. "Two little lovebirds sitting in a tree. K-I-S-S-I-N-G." You hated it when I sang that song, didn't you? *(David's older brother KYLE ENTERS.)*

KYLE: I figured you'd be here. Mom and Dad were wondering about you. When did you get into town?

DAVID: A few hours ago. I had to check into the motel.

KYLE: Mom wishes you'd stay at the house.

DAVID: I never do.

KYLE: She was hoping this time you'd change your mind.

DAVID: It's nothing personal. I just like... need my space.

KYLE: Mom and Dad thought we'd all come here tonight. As a family.

DAVID: I know. You always do. I didn't forget.

KYLE: But you never come with us. You always come here alone.

DAVID: Can you blame me?

KYLE: David, it's been eight years.

DAVID: *(Snaps.)* Don't you think I know that?

KYLE: Maybe it's time for you to join the family in remembering Timmy, instead of doing it all alone.

DAVID: It's just easier this way.

KYLE: Maybe easier for you. Harder for Mom and Dad.

DAVID: I know.

KYLE: So?

DAVID: So I don't think I can make it. I'm doing my own thing here, just like I do every year. It shouldn't surprise them.

KYLE: No. But it makes them even sadder.

DAVID: Thanks. Like I need more guilt heaped on me.

KYLE: You need to let go of the guilt.

DAVID: Catch you back at the house, okay?

KYLE: You'll be there for dinner?

DAVID: Always am.

KYLE: Just reconsider. It would mean the world to Mom and Dad if you'd come here with us tonight. You still can do your private thing now. But come back tonight with the family.

DAVID: I don't get it. I never do. Why do they want me there? I'm the son who killed his brother.

KYLE: Because they love you. It was an accident. When are you going to forgive yourself?

DAVID: I don't know. Maybe never.

KYLE: Everyone else has forgiven you, including Mom and Dad. *(Pause.)* You were sixteen. A kid yourself.

DAVID: A sixteen-year-old who thought he was invincible.

KYLE: Didn't we all think that at that age?

DAVID: But we didn't all kill our brother!

KYLE: David, it was an accident!

DAVID: *(Snaps.)* Peeling out of the driveway like a bad ass and ramming my car into my little brother! Reckless! Stupid! Call it what you want, but it was my fault! I stormed out of the house, because I was pissed off that Dad was making me take out the garbage! I killed my brother over taking out the trash. How stupid was that?! I tore out of there and never— *(Pauses abruptly.)* —never looked back.

KYLE: You were a kid.

DAVID: No! Timmy was a kid! He was ten years old. I was a dumb teenager with no respect for my parents. And to this day, I can't look Mom in the eye, knowing what I did.

KYLE: You made a mistake.

DAVID: A mistake? That's what you call killing your little brother?

KYLE: You would never hurt Timmy on purpose. Everyone knows that.

DAVID: I'd switch places with him right now if I could.

KYLE: Everyone knows that. Mom and Dad are worried about you. I am too. We all are.

DAVID: I'm fine.

KYLE: No, you're not. You need to let go of this guilt and come back to the family.

DAVID: I said I'd be there for dinner tonight.

KYLE: You know what I mean.

DAVID: It's just easier this way. I'd rather grieve alone.

KYLE: But maybe a family needs to do this together. It's been eight years, David. Can't you find it in your heart to come back? And by that, I mean, really connect with us again. We miss you. Mom especially. She feels like she's lost you too.

DAVID: Why can't you understand?

KYLE: Understand what?

DAVID: I killed our little brother! Me! I put him here in the ground! Me! It was all my fault! He should be graduating from high school this year, but I ended his life! He's in that grave because of me!

KYLE: Stop it! Timmy admired you more than anyone else in the family. More than me, Mom, Dad. He knows you'd never hurt him for anything. And you wouldn't. He would be so sad right now if he knew how miserable you still were. Don't you know that? Remember how he would stand at your bedroom door and knock and knock if he thought you were holed up in there upset about something? He'd slide notes under the door. Sometimes candy. He couldn't stand for you to be sad. Remember?

DAVID: I remember.

KYLE: So you need to think about that. Remember him knocking on your bedroom door. "David, open up. Let me in." And you always gave in to him. You'd say, "Get in here, dork. But stay on that side of the room." But before long, you two would be laughing and wrestling on the floor until Mom screamed for you to pipe down.

DAVID: He was a great brother.

KYLE: So were you. You know he'd be knocking on your door right now if he could.

DAVID: Even though I killed him?

KYLE: Especially then. He couldn't stand it when you were sad.

DAVID: It's just so hard. I miss him so much.

KYLE: We all do. But you had a special connection with Timmy that none of us had with him. So, you need to step it up and let him see you happy again. Please? Will you try? For Timmy?

DAVID: *(Nods.)* Yeah. I guess so. I wouldn't want him worrying about me.

KYLE: That's right. So, come on. Let's go home for dinner.

DAVID: Okay. For Timmy. *(As they EXIT, the GROUNDSKEEPER ENTERS and crosses to Timmy's grave.)*

GROUNDSKEEPER: I don't know what happened, little guy, but I can tell you this. Your big brother loves you more than he can say. So, I'd say you're one lucky fellow. See you tomorrow, Timmy.

SPARE CHANGE

SYNOPSIS: A young professional woman tries to help a mentally ill homeless woman who has often caught her attention.

CAST: 2F
   Emily (mid-20s)
   Polly (40s or older)

SETTING: City sidewalk in a downtown area
PROPS: Purse, coins

EMILY, a professionally dressed young woman, approaches POLLY, a homeless woman who has often caught EMILY'S attention from across the street where she works. She has finally managed to find the courage to approach this woman, mostly out of curiosity, but also with a desire to help her. POLLY wears mismatched clothes and sits on the sidewalk, happily humming a made-up tune.

EMILY: *(Approaching.)* Hello.

POLLY: Oh, hi.

EMILY: I was wondering... *(Reaches into her purse.)* Do you need some money? I'm actually low on cash right now, but... *(Digs to the bottom of her purse.)* I have some spare change.

POLLY: I don't need any money.

EMILY: Please take it. *(Offers her the change.)*

POLLY: *(Takes the coins.)* Your choice.

EMILY: I'm sorry it's not more. I'm terrible about carrying cash on me. I mean, if I have it, I spend it. Thank goodness for debit cards.

POLLY: "You must save before you spend to begin a trend. Otherwise you shall spend without an end."

EMILY: That's good advice. I need to save more. But everything is so expensive these days. It's hard to get ahead. *(Pause as she tries to think of something else to say.)* I work across the street. *(Points.)* Over there. At the Martin Davis Law Firm. I notice you here every day.

POLLY: *(Indifferent to Emily's statement.)* Would you like to sit down?

EMILY: Well, I... *(Considers how she can do this in her outfit.)* Sure. *(Flips off her heels and sits next to POLLY.)* I'm Emily.

POLLY: Hello, Emily. I'm Polly.

EMILY: It's nice to meet you, Polly.

POLLY: *(After a moment of awkward silence.)* What do you do at the law office?

EMILY: I'm a paralegal. My firm handles a lot of family law cases.

POLLY: Divorces?

EMILY: Yes. Divorces. Custody battles.

POLLY: Sounds depressing. You should look for another job.

EMILY: Oh, I like my job.

POLLY: Divorces are not a good thing.

EMILY: No, they're not. And you're right. It's sad to watch these marriages fall apart on a day-to-day basis.

POLLY: Does your firm tell them to work it out? Get counseling?

EMILY: No. Unfortunately, that's not our job. Besides, most of our clients are spewing hatred for their soon-to-be ex. Which is sad knowing they were once madly in love. It's rare to see a peaceful divorce.

POLLY: You should tell them about the fruits of the spirit.

EMILY: The what?

POLLY: The fruits of the spirit. Joy, peace, patience, kindness, goodness, faithfulness, gentleness, and self-control.

EMILY: I don't think that would go over well. Especially if my boss heard me preaching to our clients. Not that those aren't good qualities to have, but I'd get in trouble for that.

POLLY: Have the clients create a peace collage. Pictures of images that make them feel relaxed and at ease. It will calm their souls.

EMILY: I don't think my boss would approve of that either. He's pretty... let's just say... hard-nosed. You know, tough, focused, and sometimes ruthless. Those are good attributes for an attorney. If I needed an attorney I'd want him to be like that.

POLLY: All it takes is magazines, scissors, construction paper, and glue to make a collage.

EMILY: My role in the process is being the sympathizer. I spend hours on the phone listening to people bad mouth their exes and cry. They do a lot of crying. I suppose there are days that I don't like my job. I don't think I've ever admitted that to anyone before. Except to you. Maybe I should look for something else to do.

POLLY: *(Out of nowhere.)* Do you know what the four best agricultural states are?

EMILY: Wow, no. I don't know that.

POLLY: California, Texas, Iowa, and Nebraska.

EMILY: That's interesting. So, Polly, where are you from?

POLLY: I'm from up north.

EMILY: Oh, where?

POLLY: Minnesota.

EMILY: Do you have family here?

POLLY: No. They're all in Minnesota. Two brothers. And one sister-in-law.

EMILY: That's nice. Do they know where you are?

POLLY: Yes. I send them Christmas cards.

EMILY: How did you end up here? So far away from your family?

POLLY: I came here because it's warm. I don't like the cold.

EMILY: I don't either. I'm not a winter person. *(Looks around the area.)* So, where exactly do you live?

POLLY: I live here.

EMILY: Here?

POLLY: *(Motions behind her.)* This is my home.

EMILY: But... where's all your stuff? Your belongings?

POLLY: The shopping cart over there. That's my stuff.

EMILY: But this isn't a safe place to live.

POLLY: *(Stands.)* I need to stretch my legs.

EMILY: *(Stands.)* Me too. *(Looks at watch.)* I have to get back to work soon. But I have a few more minutes. *(Pause.)* So, have you ever worked anywhere?

POLLY: I worked at the Union Rescue Mission.

EMILY: Really?

POLLY: Yes. Mostly I answered the phones. Like you.

EMILY: So how did you end up... here?

POLLY: Do you want some canned beets? They're highly nutritious. I have some leftover from lunch.

EMILY: Where did you get canned beets?

POLLY: The manager of Quick Mart sometimes gives me something. If it's gone past its expiration date.

EMILY: Oh. *(Pause.)* No, thank you on the beets. I had a cheeseburger a while ago.

POLLY: You should eat beets. You should eat them every day.

EMILY: Sorry. I guess I'm really not a fan of beets.

POLLY: Do you have a boyfriend?

EMILY: *(Caught off guard.)* Huh?

POLLY: Do you have a boyfriend?

EMILY: Not at the moment.

POLLY: I know who your Mr. Right is.

EMILY: You do?

POLLY: Yes. Dr. Turner. He's an ophthalmologist. He gave me these glasses.

EMILY: Well, I don't know Dr. Turner, but I'm sure he's nice.

POLLY: He's slender, tall, and has thick grayish hair. His soothing vox will appeal to you.

EMILY: His vox? What is that?

POLLY: His voice. Vox is Latin for voice.

EMILY: You're very smart, Polly.

POLLY: Dr. Turner has an office on Tower Drive. East of Meadow. Go make an appointment with him.

EMILY: Oh, I don't think so. I'm not looking for anyone right now. Actually, I'm taking a sabbatical from men. I've been burned too many times.

POLLY: Did you take advanced algebra?

EMILY: Algebra? *(Thinks.)* Did I take advanced algebra? Yes. I barely passed. And the only reason I passed was 'cause I had a tutor. And my boyfriend beat me over the head with the equations until they somehow stuck. Why do you ask?

POLLY: Algebra aids agronomists, architects, and artists.

EMILY: Interesting. But I'm not sure what an agronomist is.

POLLY: A crop scientist.

EMILY: Polly, you're too intelligent to be— *(Stops herself.)* I just don't understand how you ended up living on the streets.

POLLY: If you have any fractions, get rid of those first by multiplying all items by the lowest common denominator.

EMILY: I don't remember any of that stuff. In fact, I chose to forget it.

POLLY: Your ultimate goal is to get all of the constants on one side of the equation and all the variables on the other side of the equation.

EMILY: Polly—

POLLY: Do you want me to show you some examples?

EMILY: Do you want me to help you find a place to live?

POLLY: No. I like it here.

EMILY: But wouldn't you like to have a warm, safe place to live?

POLLY: I don't want to live in a house. I like living here.

EMILY: What about a small apartment? Do you have any income? I know they offer affordable housing for people who have a limited income. Maybe I could find some resources to help you.

POLLY: My friend Jan lives in one of those apartments for low-income people.

EMILY: Well, see? It would be perfect for you.

POLLY: No. I'm safer here. Jan has to board up all of her windows because of all of the drug dealers. They'll break into your apartment and steal everything you have or kill you.

EMILY: I'm sure that's just an exaggeration. If you lock your doors—

POLLY: When she gets home from work, she's in fear for her life. She tells me that. Sometimes she doesn't even want to go home, so she stays here with me. It's much safer here where I live.

EMILY: Where does she work?

POLLY: At Quick Mart. She bags groceries. And you know what else? She knows someone who was killed at those apartments. Mary Lee Walker. They killed her over just a few dollars.

EMILY: Well, maybe you could live in a different apartment complex. There are others.

POLLY: No. I feel safe here.

EMILY: Even at night? When it's dark?

POLLY: Its hue is green, beryl, mint, or teal.

EMILY: What is?

POLLY: London blue topaz.

EMILY: Polly...

POLLY: Have you ever seen London blue topaz?

EMILY: I want to help you.

POLLY: Hey, have you heard this song? *(Hums.)*

EMILY: No, I don't believe I have.

POLLY: Listen. *(Hums again.)*

EMILY: It doesn't sound familiar.

POLLY: Come on. You know it. *(Hums.)*

EMILY: No, I don't.

POLLY: It's a song by Don Crawford. He plays the trumpet.

EMILY: I'm sorry, but I don't—

POLLY: Listen! *(Hums louder.)*

EMILY: *(Speaks over POLLY'S humming.)* I have to get back to work now. But I'm going to see what I can do to help you find a home. Even in the south we have miserable winters with ice and freezing cold temperatures. I'd hate to see you exposed to such conditions. There's no reason you shouldn't be safe and warm. I can make some phone calls. My friend Kelly volunteers at the Salvation Army. I'm sure she could steer me in the right direction. I want to help you. You shouldn't have to live like this. No one should.

POLLY: Did you like it?

EMILY: Did you hear what I just said?

POLLY: Do you want to hear it again?

EMILY: Listen, Polly. I want to help you. My friend volunteers at the Salvation Army, and I think—

POLLY: It's in the key of A. It sounds like spring.

EMILY: Don't you want a bed to sleep in at night?

POLLY: I want to play the trumpet. *(Demonstrates playing the trumpet.)*

EMILY: You're not listening to me. I'm trying to help you.

POLLY: Can you drive me to the music store?

EMILY: Why?

POLLY: I want to buy a trumpet. I have some money. *(Digs through her pockets to find coins and shows them to Emily.)* See. I have money.

EMILY: *(Touches her arm.)* Polly...

POLLY: My name is Loretta.

EMILY: But you said it was Polly.

POLLY: You may call me Loretta. May I call you Terry?

EMILY: I'm Emily. My name is Emily. Listen, Polly—

POLLY: I'm Loretta.

EMILY: Loretta, I think you need some help. Maybe you should see a doctor.

POLLY: I don't need a doctor. I'm in good health. I eat asparagus. It protects you from cancer. Do you eat it?

EMILY: No. I hate asparagus. In fact, I hate most vegetables. Except for potatoes. And I usually eat those in the form of french fries.

POLLY: Lemons reduce your risk of stroke. *(Starts "playing" the trumpet again.)*

EMILY: If I made you an appointment with a special doctor, would you go? *(POLLY ignores her.)* Sometimes people need help. And there are medications to help people feel better. You know, feel less foggy. Less confused. Peaceful.

POLLY: Don't forget about the peace collage I told you about.

EMILY: No, I won't. So will you go?

POLLY: To buy a trumpet?

EMILY: To see a doctor. I'm going to make you an appointment. I'll go with you too. It could be fun. Like a girls' day out.

POLLY: No! No doctors!

EMILY: There's no need to be afraid. I'll be there.

POLLY: No! No! I don't need a doctor. I don't like doctors.

EMILY: You like Dr. Turner. He's a doctor.

POLLY: He gave me these glasses.

EMILY: And that was nice of him, wasn't it? I'll find you a nice doctor like him, Polly.

POLLY: My name's Loretta. Why do you keep calling me Polly? *(Starts pacing.)* Detox. Detox. Detox the mind.

EMILY: There's a Professional Care Center by the hospital, and I can call and make you an appointment.

POLLY: Breathe.

EMILY: I'll go with you. And afterwards we can go to the Salvation Army. I'm sure we can get you some help there. And some different clothes too. And maybe you can stay at the Salvation Army until there's an apartment available. See, Polly—I mean, Loretta, it's a good thing that we met. I'm going to help you.

POLLY: *(Still pacing.)* Detox. Breathe. Detox. Breathe.

EMILY: I'm sure it's all a bit frightening, but I'll be there with you. First we'll see a doctor—

POLLY: No doctors. No more doctors!

EMILY: Polly—

POLLY: Loretta! My name is Loretta!

EMILY: Ok. I'm sorry. Loretta.

POLLY: No doctor. No apartment. This is my home. Two thumbs up.

EMILY: The street is no place to live. You aren't safe here. And if you see a doctor who can... you know... fix things up here... *(Touches her head.)* Then you'll feel better.

POLLY: You may go.

EMILY: You want me to leave?

POLLY: I have things to do.

EMILY: I'm trying to help... *(Looks at her watch.)* Oh my gosh! I'm late! I need to get back to work. But I can come back tomorrow if you want me to.

POLLY: Don't be late. You need to go.

EMILY: I'll come back tomorrow. Okay? I'm sorry. Maybe it was too much too soon. Yes, I think it was. Do you want me to bring you a cheeseburger tomorrow? We could have a picnic together. Right here.

POLLY: Cut the pickles. I don't like pickles. Too acidic.

EMILY: Okay. I'll cut the pickles. I'll see you tomorrow. *(Pauses to see if she will say goodbye.)* Bye, Loretta. *(POLLY does not look at her, but pretends she is playing the trumpet as EMILY EXITS.)*

⟫JUDGES⟫

SYNOPSIS: Gossiping women attack the subject of their latest rumors, only to be confronted with the truth.

CAST: 4F
  Kim (30)
  Dana (26)
  Blair (28)
  Isabelle (32)

SETTING: Hospital employee breakroom
PROPS: Counter or table, coffee pot, mugs, cell phone

KIM and DANA ENTER the employee breakroom at the hospital where they work. They each pour a cup of coffee.

KIM: I'm telling you, she's on her third or fourth marriage.

DANA: Are you serious?

KIM: Yes. And I think all of her kids have different fathers.

DANA: That's terrible. Who would do that to their kids?

KIM: I wouldn't. *(BLAIR, a oo workor, ENTERS.)*

BLAIR: *(Pours a cup of coffee.)* Hey, Kim. Hi, Dana. What a morning this has been! I need coffee.

DANA: We had the same thought. Hospital madness today.

KIM: *(Back to DANA.)* Oh, and have you noticed how she dresses?

DANA: Her skirts are too short, if you ask me.

BLAIR: Who are you talking about?

KIM: Isabelle in public relations.

DANA: Did you know she's on her fourth or fifth marriage?

BLAIR: I don't believe that's true. And even if it is, who cares?

DANA: I'm just saying, she's messed up.

BLAIR: Aren't we all a little messed up?

DANA: Not like her. And speaking of which, I noticed she stopped wearing her wedding ring last week.

KIM: Really? Do you think she's going through another divorce?

DANA: That would be my guess.

KIM: I bet she is. Now that you mention it, I have noticed Chad Corbit going in and out of her office quite a bit. I bet there's something going on between the two of them. And he's married.

DANA: Watch, he'll be the next one going through a divorce. We'll just call Isabelle "the happy homewrecker."

BLAIR: I don't believe any of this is true. And even if it was, what business is it of yours? Who are you? Her judge and jury?

KIM: Blair, we're not judging Isabelle. We're just stating the facts.

BLAIR: You don't even know the facts.

DANA: But it's interesting.

BLAIR: How's that?

DANA: Interesting how someone can mess up her life like she has. I can't help it if I happen to observe what's going on. But it does make you wonder. How can she look at herself in the mirror every morning knowing what she's doing?

BLAIR: What exactly do you think she's doing?

KIM: I know for a fact that she's been divorced several times.

BLAIR: How do you know that? Did Isabelle tell you?

KIM: No, she told Rosa.

BLAIR: And Rosa blabbed Isabelle's whole life story to you?

KIM: She just mentioned it casually at lunch last week.

DANA: And she told me Isabelle is a control freak.

KIM: Really?

DANA: Yeah. She said if she picks up her phone to send a few text messages, Isabelle gives her a dirty look.

KIM: Oh, I've seen that look.

BLAIR: Well, we have a policy prohibiting cell phones at work unless it's an emergency.

DANA: I think she walks around looking for people on their phones just so she can get them in trouble.

BLAIR: That's not true!

DANA: Short skirt girl on patrol! Everyone put away their phones!

KIM: Oh my gosh! It's like we're back in high school.

BLAIR: *(Glares at DANA and KIM.)* I agree. It's so immature to talk about people behind their back when you don't know the facts and they can't defend themselves.

ISABELLE: *(ENTERS.)* I need coffee. *(Glances around.)* It looks like we're all loading up on the caffeine today. Is this Monday, or what? *(Looks at her cell phone.)*

BLAIR: Good morning! Yes, it's definitely a Monday.

DANA: *(Indicates phone.)* Not to be rude, Isabelle, but did you forget hospital policy?

ISABELLE: Excuse me?

DANA: Phones are to be tucked away unless it's an emergency. No texting or Facebooking during work. Lives are at stake here.

KIM: But, of course, Isabelle doesn't really save lives in PR. Not like the doctors and us nurses. But still, Dr. Webster has a strict policy. So, you better put your phone away before you get caught.

ISABELLE: I'm on my break. And it is kind of an emergency. That's why I stepped away from my office to come in here.

BLAIR: Is everything okay?

ISABELLE: No. Not really. It's some legal matters.

KIM: I know a good family law attorney. Do you want his name?

ISABELLE: No, thank you.

BLAIR: Is there anything I can do?

ISABELLE: Thanks, but it's complicated.

DANA: Yep, going through a divorce is hard.

ISABELLE: I'm not going through a divorce.

DANA: Oh. Well, we just thought...

KIM: And we noticed you're not wearing your ring.

ISABELLE: You noticed I wasn't wearing my ring? Really? It's being cleaned, for your information. Gosh, from not wearing my ring to divorce. That's quite a leap. You don't think much of me, do you?

KIM: We just assumed you were going through another divorce. It doesn't mean we think you're a bad person.

ISABELLE: Another divorce? How do you even know about the divorce I went through a long time ago? A long, long time ago.

DANA: Only one?

BLAIR: Isabelle, you don't have to explain anything to them.

DANA: *(To BLAIR.)* Maybe she wants to. *(To ISABELLE.)* How many divorces have you had? Three? Four?

ISABELLE: Why would you ask me such a question?

KIM: Because we heard you've had several failed marriages. Just curious. Hey, it happens. Relationships are tough these days.

ISABELLE: You've heard? People are talking about me?

KIM: You know. People like to talk.

ISABELLE: Yes, some people do. I hear it all the time. I just had no clue that I was the latest object of gossip. That's just great. Well, for the record, I've had one divorce. And my husband and I have been married for ten years. He has a stepson who gives us plenty of challenges, but we're happy.

DANA: Really?

ISABELLE: Really.

KIM: We weren't gossiping about you.

DANA: No. We were just concerned.

ISABELLE: About?

DANA: About your image. You know, the short skirts that you wear can give men the wrong impression.

ISABELLE: Seriously? You're criticizing my clothes? Really? My husband is always complimenting my legs, so I enjoy wearing skirts that show them off a little. But I am not, let me repeat, not trying to impress anyone but my husband, and everything I wear adheres to the hospital dress code.

BLAIR: I think you look nice.

ISABELLE: Thanks.

DANA: I'm sorry. We just heard... oh, never mind.

ISABELLE: Heard what?

DANA: Nothing.

ISABELLE: What? Tell me! If I'm the object of workplace gossip, I deserve to hear what you're saying about me.

KIM: Everyone thinks you and Chad are having an affair.

ISABELLE: They think I'm having an affair with Chad?! The tech in anesthesiology?

KIM: Well, Rosa said he comes into your office a lot. Like all the time. It's okay. You can tell us.

BLAIR: Just ignore them.

ISABELLE: Rosa said that?

DANA: She's concerned about you, Isabelle. We're all concerned about you.

ISABELLE: Are you so concerned about me that you need to talk behind my back and decide what's wrong with me without asking me personally?

KIM: We thought asking you would be rude.

ISABELLE: And gossiping about me isn't?

KIM: We're only trying to share our concerns.

ISABELLE: No. You're bad mouthing me as if you know what's going on in my life.

BLAIR: They don't know anything. Except how to tear people down and start rumors. And why? Who knows why except to receive some sort of sick high from the thought that it may all be true.

ISABELLE: *(To KIM and DANA.)* So, what do you really know about me? What? What?

KIM: Nothing, I suppose.

ISABELLE: That's right. You know nothing. You only think you know something. So, let's see. You think I dress provocatively? *(KIM and DANA hesitantly nod.)*

BLAIR: They're crazy! You dress very professionally.

ISABELLE: Thank you. *(Back to KIM and DANA.)* Oh, and because my rings are being cleaned, I'm going through another divorce? What does this make? The third, fourth, or fifth divorce?

DANA: Someone told me you'd been divorced several times.

ISABELLE: Who?

KIM: People talk. And you have been through a divorce.

ISABELLE: One! One divorce, Kim. What about you? How many times have you been divorced?

KIM: Hey, leave me out of this.

ISABELLE: I heard you went through two divorces and swore you'd never get married again. But you're engaged now, right?

KIM: That's true. And yes, I've finally met my soul mate. It took me a few tries.

ISABELLE: That's wonderful. But you've been divorced more times than I have and yet you're judging me?

DANA: It's just what we heard. Relax.

ISABELLE: You think you should believe everything you hear? And even worse, spread it around as if you know it's true?

KIM: Oh, get off your high and mighty horse.

ISABELLE: Then you stop gossiping about people. About me! Stop spreading lies!

DANA: Like we said, we were just concerned.

ISABELLE: Concerned?

DANA: That's right. People were talking and—

ISABELLE: People? You were the ones talking about me.

KIM: You just said that you were going through some legal issues. You know, I'm sorry, but it does sound like you have some serious problems going on. In my experience, some people just bring it on themselves. So maybe you need to take a long, hard look in the mirror and ask yourself why. Why am I making such a mess out of my life?

DANA: Which is why you need a good friend to confide in and offer some advice. That's why I was going to invite you to lunch and offer to be a friend. Offer some advice, if you'd like.

ISABELLE: When?

DANA: Soon.

ISABELLE: Well, let's have it. Give me your advice.

DANA: Over lunch?

ISABELLE: Skip the lunch and get straight to the nitty gritty. Give me your so-called needed advice.

DANA: Uh, not with that attitude.

ISABELLE: *(Smiles.)* Please.

DANA: All right. It's very simple.

ISABELLE: I'm listening.

DANA: Sometimes when you keep repeating the same mistakes in your life, over and over, you have to take a step back and stop and look at yourself. You know, delve inside your soul and truly look at yourself. Then maybe you'll figure out that you need to go in the opposite direction.

ISABELLE: Oh. You mean stop doing stupid things and make better choices?

DANA: Yes! Exactly!

ISABELLE: Become a new person?

DANA: Yes!

ISABELLE: Change who I am?

DANA: Exactly!

KIM: Good advice, Dana.

ISABELLE: Are you ready to hear what I think?

DANA: Sure.

ISABELLE: I think you need to turn that finger back around to yourself, Dana. *(Looks at KIM.)* And you too, Kim.

BLAIR: Good advice, Isabelle.

DANA: What are you talking about?

ISABELLE: You both need to step back and look at yourselves. Delve into your souls and figure out what is going on here. Ask yourselves, "Why am I judging others who I know nothing about? To make myself feel good? Or is it just because deep down inside I'm a hateful person?" And then, you need to turn and go the opposite direction. Which means... stop! Neither of you know anything about me! Nothing! Do you hear me? Nothing. I've been happily married to my husband, Mark, for more than a decade. He bought me this skirt in New York when he was there on a business trip, because he missed me and thought it would look pretty on me. Did you know that? And did you know that my stepson, Phillip, has Down's syndrome? Did you know that? Did you? We are raising him and doing the best we can. I love Phillip. I love him as if he were my own son. His mother is the reason we are seeing an attorney. She's strung out on drugs and has it in her mind that she wants to get custody of him even though she's never been there for him. So, we've hired an attorney to represent us in court. *(Holds up her phone.)* I just missed a phone call from him, and I was going to call him back during my break. In case you needed to know. Oh! And Chad... sweet, sweet Chad, who I'm supposedly having an affair with because he comes into my office. Now, he's what I call a real friend. Did you know that his daughter is autistic? We both attend a support group for parents with children who have challenges in their lives. Sometimes he drops by my office to see what I thought of the last meeting or to ask for advice in dealing with his daughter. He also lets me vent about my own difficulties with Phillip or his mother. Yes, Chad is a true friend. Unlike the two of you. Any questions? Any advice you want to give me now from your judge's bench? *(DANA and KIM shake their heads.)* Good! *(Storms OUT.)*

BLAIR: Guess she set you two straight. I hope you learned your lesson. *(EXITS.)*

DANA: I didn't know all that.

KIM: Me neither.

DANA: Guess we should apologize.

KIM: Yeah, we probably should. *(They pause thoughtfully.)*

DANA: Hey, did you see Diane this morning?

KIM: Oh my God, yes! What did she do to her hair?

DANA: No kidding! I mean, what was she thinking? *(They EXIT.)*

LOSS OF INNOCENCE

SYNOPSIS: A young woman confronts the uncle who sexually abused her as a child.

CAST: 2M, 2F
    Darla (40s)
    Sara (25)
    Sid (37)
    Lance (46)

SETTING: Therapist's office
PROPS: Couch, three chairs

DARLA, a therapist, talks to her patient, SARA, who plans to face the uncle who molested her as a child.

DARLA: If you could go back, what would you do differently?

SARA: If I could go back? Why do you always ask me these hypothetical questions? I can't go back.

DARLA: Pretend.

SARA: I would run.

DARLA: Run?

SARA: Yes. I would run in the opposite direction.

DARLA: At family gatherings?

SARA: Only at night. During the day, everything was fine.

DARLA: But at night?

SARA: That's when the creepy people come out, right? Not creepy, monstrous. He was a monster.

DARLA: So it was always at night?

SARA: Yeah, the whole family was together at this big vacation house on the beach for ten days. My cousins and I would stay up late every night. And he would try to act like one of us even though he was much older. He'd say, "Let those old folks go to bed early. We'll stay up late and raid the fridge and watch scary movies."

DARLA: How old were you?

SARA: I was fourteen. He was twenty-six.

DARLA: Old enough to know better.

SARA: Yes. But wasn't I old enough to know better too? So, why didn't I stop him?

DARLA: You wanted him to like you.

SARA: I guess. Uncle Sid made me laugh. He always knew how to get down on my level. We'd have water balloon fights in the dark while everyone was sleeping. Then we'd sneak into the kitchen and share a gallon of ice cream and pour chocolate syrup all over the place. On the ice cream, our fingers, our noses. We'd be silly, and he'd tell me I was beautiful. He'd say I made his heart flutter.

DARLA: And how did that make you feel?

SARA: At the time I liked it. My relationship with my mom was very difficult, and Uncle Sid made me feel special. Loved. He'd tell me that he loved me.

DARLA: In a romantic way?

SARA: Yes. Now I realize it was wrong. He was twenty-six. He wasn't really falling in love with his fourteen-year-old niece.

DARLA: Start from the beginning.

SARA: Again? You've heard all of this before.

DARLA: I want you to go over it again.

SARA: Why?

DARLA: You know why.

SARA: *(Takes a deep breath.)* He said he loved me.

DARLA: You were a child.

SARA: Was I? I was fourteen years old. At first it was handholding. Then little kisses. Playful kisses. But then...

DARLA: Then?

SARA: I don't know.

DARLA: Yes, you do.

SARA: He would kiss me in a different way. I never liked it. I would push him away and tell him he was acting dumb. I'd say, "Stop it, Uncle Sid!" And he'd make a joke or get mad.

DARLA: What did you do when he got mad?

SARA: Don't ask me why, but I'd apologize. Is that messed up or what? When he was the one who... *(Pause.)*

DARLA: When he was the one... doing what, Sara?

SARA: Manipulating me. I guess that's why they pick on kids, huh? So they can feel powerful.

DARLA: So if you could go back, what would you do differently? Say he touched you inappropriately, and you told him to stop, but he just got mad at you. Would you say you're sorry? Apologize?

SARA: No.

DARLA: What would you say?

SARA: Stop!

DARLA: But he's mad.

SARA: I don't care! Stop it!

DARLA: Are you ready to tell him? To his face? We've been working up to this for months, and you know he's in the waiting room.

SARA: I guess. I think so. *(Pause.)* Yes, I am.

DARLA: *(Goes to the door and motions for SID.)* We're ready for you now.

SID: *(Bursts IN.)* Thanks for forcing me into this little therapy session! Just what I wanted to do on my Thursday afternoon.

DARLA: I appreciate you making the time, Sid.

SID: I had no choice. According to you, it was either this or Little Miss Drama Queen here might file charges against me. I still plan on looking into the statute of limitations.

DARLA: You do that. But as long as you're here, please, sit down.

SID: *(Points at SARA as he sits.)* It's your word against mine. You remember that!

DARLA: We appreciate you coming in.

SID: Only to put a stop to this garbage! Let's throw the trash out right here. Because I sure don't want to deal with any more lies from her. This is messing with my life, my marriage... I don't need legal problems, defending myself against her stupid lies.

SARA: Lies?! You know perfectly well what you did to me.

SID: *(To DARLA.)* She's lost her mind. *(To SARA.)* You've conjured up some sick fantasy and for some reason put my name on it. I don't know why. I'll never understand why.

SARA: You're right about one thing. It was sick.

SID: Why don't you grow up?

SARA: I did. I'm not the little girl you can control anymore. I'm ready to face you. Finally. After months of therapy. After all the shame, hating myself, feeling dirty... all because of you!

SID: *(To DARLA.)* She's nuts! Don't you get that? Nuts!

DARLA: You need to listen to her. Sara has some things to tell you.

SID: I believe she just did. You know, you should prescribe her some medications, because your therapy obviously isn't working.

SARA: You know what? I didn't think I could hate you any more, but now I do. More than ever.

SID: I'm telling you, the girl needs some meds. Or maybe she needs to be admitted to a mental hospital. Get her out of here! *(To SARA.)* You're crazy! *(There is a knock on the door.)* Who's that? More so-called abusers from her past? *(DARLA answers the door, and LANCE, Sara's father, ENTERS.)*

SARA: Dad!

DARLA: Thank you for coming.

SID: *(Nervous.)* Hey, bro! What are you doing here?

LANCE: What do you think? I'm here to support my daughter, and I have some things I need to say.

SID: What do you mean?

LANCE: This is going to end here and now. Things need to be said. And be heard.

SID: Lance, she's messed up!

LANCE: If I knew back then, I would've... Well, you wouldn't be alive right now.

SID: Why is everyone picking on me? Is this Pick on Sid Day? Why the hell is everyone accusing me of something I didn't do? I didn't do a damn thing. Except get threatened by everyone in this room. *(To DARLA.)* And you? Over the phone. "Be here or be sorry." Where do you get off as a professional making threats like that?

LANCE: I still think Sara should file charges.

SARA: Dad, we've been over this. It would drag on forever and hurt our family even more. And as long as he stays away from me...

LANCE: Oh, he'll stay away! Won't you, Sid?

SID: Lance, have you been listening to her nonsense? Her lies? Why is everyone listening to her and not me? Why does everyone believe her? It's not true. Why won't anyone listen to me?

DARLA: Sid, we've asked you to come here to listen. Sara has some things she'd like to tell you. Please listen to her.

SID: What? What do you want to tell me? What kind of bullshit do you want to tell everyone in this room? That ridiculous made-up story that I did something to you when you were a kid?

SARA: Yes, but you know I didn't make it up. It's not a lie.

SID: Oh, please!

DARLA: Go ahead, Sara.

SARA: *(Pause. To SID.)* You're scum. You took advantage of me. I was just a fourteen-year-old girl who loved her uncle and wanted him to like me. But you forced me to do things I should never have done. And for that I hated myself for years. But now I know it's you I hate. I hate you with all of my heart. You took away my innocence, my trust, and my childhood.

SID: Not me! You're crazy! Why are you doing this? You're a damn liar, that's what you are!

DARLA: Ignore him, Sara. Just go on.

SARA: I felt I was nothing. You told me that sex equaled love. And I found out the hard way that it wasn't true.

SID: Oh, come on! Blah, blah, blah, blah, blah.

LANCE: Shut up! Listen to what she has to say!

SARA: No thanks to you, over time I've learned that love equals respect. Not guilt. Not shame. Not demands. I've had to undo years of believing that I was nothing. But I know now that I was wrong to think that about myself.

SID: *(Stands.)* I don't have to stay and listen to this nonsense!

LANCE: Yes, you do!

SID: Or what?

LANCE: You're staying, Sid! You'd better or the next time we see you will be in court. So sit down!

SARA: Dad! I said—

LANCE: *(To SID.)* Sit down, you bastard!

DARLA: Okay, I think both of you—

SID: *(Sits.)* Fine. Let's get this over with. Say what you've gotta say. And make it quick.

SARA: If I could go back, you know what I would do? I'd say no. Again and again and again. I'd push you away and scream for help. I'd run the opposite direction. And never—no, not once—would I let you touch me. Mess with me, threaten me, laugh it off. It wasn't funny. Do you hear me?! It wasn't funny! It wasn't a joke. Or playful. Or love. For years, my life has been messed up because of your selfish and sick advances on me. Your games. Your confusing words. What was all that about? You didn't care about anyone but yourself. I may have been your victim who you could manipulate, but not anymore. I am a survivor. I am strong, and my memories of you and what you did to me will no longer control me. Do you hear me? Do you?

SID: I—

SARA: You are nothing to me. In my mind, I can easily step on you as if you were nothing. Because I have risen above this while you have sunk lower with your unrepentant sins. So, let's see who is a prisoner of their memories now. It isn't me. *(Pause.)* May we never see each other again! *(EXITS.)*

REMEMBER ME?

SYNOPSIS: A young woman returns to her old high school, hopeful that the teacher she had a crush on ten years ago still remembers her.

CAST: 1M, 1F
   Audra (27)
   David (34)

SETTING: High school classroom

PROPS: Desk, chair, red pen, stack of papers, spiral notebook, student desk and chair

AUDRA LONG stands tentatively in the doorway of a classroom at the high school she once attended. DAVID SHORE, a teacher, sits at his desk grading papers.

DAVID: *(Notices AUDRA out of the corner of his eye.)* Just one moment. I just want to finish this last paper. *(Writes.)* Imaginative. Vivid. Personal. Watch spelling errors. *(Places the assignment in a stack on his desk. To AUDRA, still not looking directly at her.)* You must be here for a parent-teacher conference. *(Opens a spiral book.)* What period do I have your student?

AUDRA: Fifth period.

DAVID: Student's name?

AUDRA: Audra Long.

DAVID: *(Turning pages in the book.)* Audra Long. Name sounds familiar. But I don't see... fifth period. Does she go by a nickname?

AUDRA: No. *(With meaning.)* Audra Long.

DAVID: I'm not seeing an Audra Long. Are you sure Audra is in my fifth period class? Classic Literature?

AUDRA: Fifth period. 2006. *(Change the year to reflect ten years ago.)*

DAVID: *(Looks up and takes notice of AUDRA for the first time.)* 2006?! Ten years ago? I don't understand.

AUDRA: It was me. I was in your fifth period class in 2006. Poetry Appreciation.

DAVID: Wow. I'm sorry. I thought you were a parent, but now it makes sense. You look too young to be the parent of one of my high school students. 2006, huh? That was just my first or second year of teaching.

AUDRA: *(Smiles brightly.)* Do you remember me now?

DAVID: *(He doesn't.)* Let me say, it's always a pleasure to see a former student of mine. I hardly recognize you. After all, it's been ten years.

AUDRA: You don't remember me, do you?

DAVID: No, I don't. I'm sorry.

AUDRA: Really? *(Moves into the classroom and sits in a front row desk.)* I sat right here. Front row. My hair was longer back then. And I had bangs.

DAVID: You said Audra Long?

AUDRA: *(Hopeful.)* Yes. Ring any bells?

DAVID: *(Shakes his head.)* No. I'm sorry. That was a few thousand students ago.

AUDRA: *(Disappointed.)* I suppose so.

DAVID: Maybe you can refresh my memory. Tell me something about the class you were in. Besides where you sat.

AUDRA: Hmmm... okay. Well, Joey Mitchell was in this class. Do you remember him?

DAVID: The name sounds familiar.

AUDRA: Joey sat in the very back. He wasn't the best student, but he always made everyone laugh. One day he opened up a can of sardines and proceeded to pop them in his mouth like they were Tic Tacs. Everyone complained about the smell.

DAVID: I remember that!

AUDRA: You do?

DAVID: Yeah! I asked him to stop being rude eating in front of everybody else. That if he was going to eat, he needed to share his food.

AUDRA: Yep, that's what you said! And Joey, smiling from ear to ear, held up his can of sardines. "Anyone want one?"

But of course, no one did. The entire class was moaning about the smell and begging you to make him throw them away. But you walked right back there, picked up a sardine between two fingers, and popped it in your mouth.

DAVID: *(Chuckles.)* Yes, I remember. How could I forget? Joey was the only student I've ever had who brought sardines to class.

AUDRA: *(Laughs.)* Everyone started laughing. They couldn't believe you actually took a sardine!

DAVID: *(Shakes his head.)* Joey Mitchell. What a character he was. I remember. *(Points.)* He sat right back there. Always leaning his chair back against the wall. But always paying attention. I have to give him that. No, he wasn't the best student. But I certainly won't forget him. I wonder where he is now.

AUDRA: *(Stands.)* But you don't remember me? I sat right here. Got the highest grade in the class.

DAVID: Front row. I know, I should remember you. But I've had so many students over the years.

AUDRA: You often called on me during class. "Audra, who was the poet who wrote 'Wild Nights'"?

DAVID: Good question. Do you still remember?

AUDRA: Of course. Emily Dickinson. "Might I but moor tonight with thee!" She was my favorite poet back then.

DAVID: Yes, that had to be Poetry Appreciation. Too bad the school doesn't offer that class any more. *(Small laugh.)* Nowadays, I don't think kids appreciate classic poetry anyway. They're more into rap.

AUDRA: But you try to sneak it into your lessons still, right?

DAVID: Not so much. But if it makes you feel better, I still read poetry on my own. I just don't teach it. *(Pause.)* Audra, I'm sorry I don't remember you. You have to understand, I have about a hundred fifty students each semester. Over ten years, that's thousands of kids I've taught.

AUDRA: Well, you should know, I never forgot you.

DAVID: Thank you. I must have made quite an impression on you.

AUDRA: I guess that's bound to happen when you're seventeen years old. A young, handsome teacher…

an impressionable teen. And of course there was this enormous crush I had on you.

DAVID: You had a crush on me? Well, I'll take that as a compliment. Thank you again.

AUDRA: I even followed in your path. I also became a teacher.

DAVID: You did? That's wonderful! What do you teach?

AUDRA: English, of course. But unlike you, I slip poetry into my lesson plans. Sometimes I even catch myself repeating things you used to say. "Poetry is a way to celebrate the beauty of both sound and sense."

DAVID: Wow, you do remember.

AUDRA: Absolutely.

DAVID: What else do you remember?

AUDRA: "Poetry rewards an open ear and mind."

DAVID: "It triggers our senses."

AUDRA: "It spans emotions from hate and despair to admiration and adulation."

DAVID: *(Laughs.)* Wow. No wonder you were my star student.

AUDRA: It was my favorite class, and you were my favorite teacher.

DAVID: And I can't even remember you. I'm sorry.

AUDRA: Like you said, you've had thousands of students since then.

DAVID: Audra, I feel honored to know that I touched you in a way that motivated you to follow on this noble path.

AUDRA: You opened up a new world for me.

DAVID: I'm glad you could appreciate it. Honestly, most students feel like teachers shove poetry down their throats.

AUDRA: True, which only limits their understanding and enjoyment of it.

DAVID: But you understand poetry.

AUDRA: Yes. "The most concentrated form of literature. Immediate and intense."

DAVID: "Penetrating your heart and mind."

AUDRA: For not remembering who I am, we seem to have found a connection.

DAVID: Again, I'm honored to hear I made a positive impact on your life.

AUDRA: I suppose you don't remember the day I stormed into your class with tears running down my face?

DAVID: Sorry, no. Teaching high school, that's not exactly a rare occurrence.

AUDRA: You were so kind and supportive and told me everything would be all right. You were the only person in the entire world who I thought sincerely cared about me.

DAVID: What about your parents?

AUDRA: I was seventeen. I thought they were trying to ruin my life. But you were kind and gentle. On top of that, you introduced me to my love for poetry. *(Laughs.)* I wrote some horrible poetry too.

DAVID: Good or bad, I'm sure it served its purpose and enabled you to express your feelings.

AUDRA: Yes. The passions of my heart. *(A confession.)* They were all about you.

DAVID: Me?

AUDRA: I was in love with you.

DAVID: *(Uncomfortable laugh.)* Those teen years will mess you up, won't they? All those crazy feelings. And the hormones. Raging like a storm.

AUDRA: For ten years I have been in love with you.

DAVID: *(A pause. He's not sure what to say. Struggles for something.)* You know, people often confuse infatuation with love.

AUDRA: No, it was real. It still is.

DAVID: *(Again, he doesn't know what to say. Struggling.)* Audra, I'm sure it seemed real back then. Just like Joey Mitchell wanted to be noticed. So what did he do? He ate sardines during the middle of my class. Disgusting or not. And you... you wanted to be loved. And there you were, front row of my class. So, I became the target of your affection. Sensible or not.

AUDRA: But my feelings for you never disappeared.

DAVID: So are you here to face your demons? Your past?

AUDRA: Something like that.

DAVID: *(Struggling for the right words.)* And we're both a bit older.

AUDRA: Yes. Ten years older.

DAVID: Older and wiser.

AUDRA: I often dreamed of the day I could walk back into your classroom. But this time... as an adult, not a student.

DAVID: And?

AUDRA: And you would look up at me and smile...

DAVID: I'm sorry that didn't happen. I was confused.

AUDRA: ...and you would remember me.

DAVID: Again, I'm sorry.

AUDRA: And then, there would be this instant chemistry between the two of us. And it would be appropriate now, not like back then.

DAVID: Back then? Oh, no! Never! That would be wrong!

AUDRA: I know that now. But back then... It's so funny to think about it now. *(Sits back down in the chair.)* How I spent so many days sitting right here. Front row. Gazing into your eyes and convincing myself that you were as in love with me as I was with you. But I was your student.

DAVID: Which would never have happened. Never.

AUDRA: Yes, I understand that now. Time had to pass.

DAVID: And time heals. Thank goodness for that.

AUDRA: But after all this time, I had to come back and see you.

DAVID: And here you are.

AUDRA: Yes. Here I am.

DAVID: Audra...

AUDRA: *(Anxious.)* Yes?

DAVID: You have to understand that this is unexpected for me. You've had ten years to replay this dream, and I've had five minutes. It's just so... unexpected.

AUDRA: I know, David... *(Stops herself.)* Wow. That's the first time I've called you by your first name. Before it was always Mr. Shore.

DAVID: *(Tries to make a joke.)* They still call me that.

AUDRA: David, I've waited so long. Don't ruin this for me.

DAVID: Ruin this?

AUDRA: I have the perfect scene in my head. The way it's supposed to play out.

DAVID: Do you want to clue me in?

AUDRA: I don't want to deal with rejection.

DAVID: Audra, I realize that you're no longer seventeen.

AUDRA: No. I'm an adult now.

DAVID: Which means you have to look at the reality of this situation. I don't know you. And if you're honest with yourself, you don't know me either.

AUDRA: You're right. You don't know me, do you?

DAVID: No, I don't. It's as if we're total strangers, meeting for the first time.

AUDRA: *(Sudden realization.)* We are, aren't we? Oh my God. Oh, what have I done? Suddenly, I feel like crawling under a rock.

DAVID: Don't be embarrassed. Coming here today was probably something you needed to do. Something you had to do so you could let go of it.

AUDRA: Let go of you. Oh, I'm so sorry. You probably think I had a miserable childhood, and that's how all of this happened. But it wasn't like that. I had such a passion for what you taught me. And for you. I can't explain it, and I don't understand it. I graduated, I went to college, I dated. I did all the normal things any young adult would do, yet... I couldn't forget about you. I thought... I thought I was in love with you.

DAVID: Dreams can often seem so real. Like poetry and the way the words come alive in our minds. But they're still words. And when dreams feel real, it's only in your head.

AUDRA: Yes, this has all just been in my head. And I wouldn't let it go. Now here I am trying to force something from my head into reality. Something's wrong with that. With me. I'm suddenly... completely humiliated. I'm so sorry.

DAVID: Don't be ashamed. You just unintentionally got caught up in a dream, forgetting that it was just that. A dream.

AUDRA: Let's just say you were my first crush and you broke my heart.

DAVID: I'm sorry I broke your heart.

AUDRA: It wasn't your fault. You actually had nothing to do with it. Isn't that funny? And sad at the same time. You know, I think I could write a poem about all of these emotions, which seem quite overwhelming right now.

DAVID: You still write poetry?

AUDRA: Yes.

DAVID: A wonderful outlet.

AUDRA: A poem of unrequited love.

DAVID: Don't beat yourself up.

AUDRA: *(Laughs.)* All of this… ten years… and you don't even remember me.

DAVID: It doesn't mean I don't want to.

AUDRA: Huh?

DAVID: Remember you. I mean now. Get to know you.

AUDRA: Really?

DAVID: We do share one unusual passion.

AUDRA: Poetry. And also teaching.

DAVID: That's two things in common. A great place to start.

AUDRA: *(Smiles. Offers her hand.)* Audra Long. High school English teacher. Sandburg High School.

DAVID: *(Shakes her hand.)* David Shore. Nice to meet you.

NOT GOOD ENOUGH

SYNOPSIS: Two teenage brothers, one of whom has a stutter, contemplate running away from home and their verbally abusive father.

CAST: 3M
> Brad (18)
> Luke (16)
> John (late 40s)

SETTING: Backyard of a suburban house
PROPS: Bottle of glass cleaner, roll of paper towels

Brothers BRAD and LUKE are outside washing a window, hoping to please their father, JOHN, who always demands perfection from his sons. To make things worse, LUKE struggles with stuttering, which is aggravated by his father's harsh treatment.

BRAD: *(Examining the window they just cleaned.)* Looks good to me. What do you think?

LUKE: He'll say it h-h-h-has s-s-s-streaks.

BRAD: I know, but man, we've sprayed and wiped this window a hundred times. We even tried using newspaper. So there's a few streaks. That's what windows do. It really depends on where you're standing when you look at it. From here, I'd say it looks pretty good. But if you move over here... *(Walks to another place.)* ...the sun hits the window from a different angle, and then... well, I guess it doesn't look as good. But he won't notice.

LUKE: He'll say it's ba-ba-ba-bad.

BRAD: Hand me the glass cleaner. One more time for you, Daddy-oh. Like we really want to get yelled at again.

LUKE: You-you-you spray. I'll wipe. *(They work hard to clean the window, spraying, wiping, then stepping back to examine their work. They touch up a few spots here and there. JOHN ENTERS and approaches. He is angry and barbarous in the treatment of his sons. Not just today, but every day.)*

JOHN: Damn it! Aren't you done yet? Are we having a garden party here?

LUKE: Um... how-how-how does it lo-lo-look?

BRAD: What do you think, Dad? Stand over here and tell me what you think. *(Tries to lead JOHN to the place that shows the least streaks. Pause as JOHN glares at the window.)*

LUKE: G-g-g-good?

JOHN: What the hell? It looks like crap! Look at those streaks!

BRAD: We went over it a million times. I don't think it's possible to get it a hundred percent streak-free unless you want to hire a couple of professional window washers.

LUKE: The s-s-s-sun makes it look... ba-ba-ba-bad.

JOHN: You boys make it look BA-BA-BA-BAD! Always the same story! *(In a girl's tone.)* "But we tried! We tried to do what you asked. But it was hard!" I don't want to hear your sissy excuses! *(Picks up the roll of paper towels.)* Did you even use the glass cleaner? Or did you just hose it off and call it good?

BRAD: Yes, we cleaned it with glass cleaner! Look at the bottle. It's practically empty! We went over it like a hundred times.

JOHN: *(In a girl's tone.)* "We went over it like a hundred times."

LUKE: It's the s-s-s-sun. The-the-the glare.

JOHN: Damn it! When are you going to stop that stupid stuttering?

BRAD: You know he can't help it.

JOHN: Yes, he can! If I tell him to stop, then he needs to stop! *(To LUKE, in his face.)* So, stop, damn it! Stop! You're making yourself sound like a fool!

BRAD: Dad, you've been telling him that since he was five. It doesn't work like that. He can't help it. You know that.

JOHN: Don't you talk to me like that. *(Girl's tone.)* "He can't help it. I can't help it. We did our best. We tried." I'm sick of all the whining and lame excuses. If it wasn't for your mother, you both would be out on the street.

LUKE: S-S-Sorry.

JOHN: *(Puts his finger in Luke's chest.)* I just want to know when you're going to start acting like a man. When are you going to stop sounding so stupid and afraid of everything? It's time to grow up!

BRAD: Dad, stop it!

LUKE: Y-y-yes, s-s-sir.

JOHN: *(Throws the paper towels at the window.)* Now get back to work and do this window again! And again! And again. Keep on doing it until I tell you it's finished!

BRAD: Are you serious? We've been out here all afternoon already.

JOHN: And you'll stay out here all night if that's what it takes. Got it?

LUKE: Yes, s-s-sir. G-g-g-got it.

BRAD: But, Dad, I have plans with Nicole tonight.

JOHN: Well, that's just too bad for you, isn't it? Because I have different plans for you tonight.

BRAD: But it's her birthday. We're planning a surprise party for her at Milo's, and I'm the one bringing her. She thinks we're going out for a nice dinner, but we're all going to be there for the party. Everyone's at the restaurant right now decorating. I can't miss this.

JOHN: Should've thought about that before you did such a crappy job on the windows. Both of you, get back to work!

LUKE: I-I-I can do it by my-my-myself. He c-c-c-can go.

JOHN: Ha! You can't do anything by yourself. You're going to do it together, so get to work!

BRAD: *(Picks up the paper towels. In a moment of anger, he throws them at the window.)* Do it yourself! I'm not missing my girlfriend's party!

JOHN: That's it! Now you've done it! Pick it up! Do you hear me? I said, pick it up! NOW!

BRAD: *(Reluctantly, he picks up the paper towels.)* Nothing is ever good enough for you, is it?

JOHN: It would be if you'd do what I tell you to do. And now with that attitude, you can pull all the weeds when you're finished with the window. Look at all these weeds. Why, there's hundreds of them. Front and back!

LUKE: B-B-Brad has a party. I-I-I'll do everything. Front and b-b-back.

JOHN: You'll both do it 'cause I say so. So get to work. *(EXITS.)*

BRAD: *(Throws the paper towels after JOHN.)* I hate that bastard!

LUKE: He's always so m-m-mad.

BRAD: He's angry at the whole frickin' world. But he takes it out on us. Especially us.

LUKE: *(Picks up the paper towels.)* M-M-Maybe it's like the way I t-t-talk. He c-c-can't help it.

BRAD: Don't make excuses for him. And don't tell me again that he's trying to raise men, not boys. I'm sick of hearing that, and I'm sick of him.

LUKE: He makes me m-m-mad too.

BRAD: Whatever happened to respect? Love? But not with him. No! It's belittle, criticize, and insult. I don't get why Mom puts up with it.

LUKE: It's n-n-not right.

BRAD: Luke, I swear I'm not going to turn out like him. An angry piece of... I'll never be like him. Never.

LUKE: I won't e-e-e-either.

BRAD: I used to think that if I did better... achieved more... tried harder... I would finally please him. But nothing's ever good enough for him. We're never good enough for him.

LUKE: No. No pleas-s-s-sing him.

BRAD: And I've decided that I'll never have kids. I'm not taking the slightest chance of morphing into that sorry excuse for a father!

LUKE: Brad, we won't be l-l-l-like him. N-n-n-never.

BRAD: I don't know why Mom doesn't divorce him. The way he yells at her... at us. He has no idea how hard we worked on this window. But why would he care? He has two slaves to do all of his work around here! "Clean those windows! Pull those weeds! Front and back! And stop whining like a couple of girls. Do it again! And again! And again if needed!" Go to hell, Dad!

LUKE: Y-y-you should move out.

BRAD: Yeah, I should now that I've graduated. But Mom and Dad are footing the bill for me to go to college here, so I thought I'd stay. *(Pause.)* But that's not the real reason I've stayed. You know why I'm still here.

LUKE: B-b-b-because of me?

BRAD: Yeah. I can't leave you here alone. But it's only one more year, then we'll both be out of here. And after that, we're never coming back.

LUKE: Except t-t-t-to see Mom.

BRAD: No, not even for that. I'll invite Mom over to my place. Or we'll meet her places. Like restaurants or the park. Anywhere she wants to see us, but I'm not coming back here.

LUKE: You don't have t-t-t-to stay here for m-m-me.

BRAD: I'm not leaving you here with that monster. You graduate next year and after that... that's it. We'll both be out of here.

JOHN: *(ENTERS, yelling.)* Why the hell are you two just standing there?

LUKE: S-s-s-sorry.

JOHN: Sorry?! Sorry doesn't cut it. Now get to work! And when you finish the windows, then it's on to the weeds. Got it? Front and back. All night long if that's what it takes. You can get a flashlight and pull, pull, pull! But be quiet about it because I don't want you waking me up.

BRAD: We'll do the window one last time. But then I need to shower and pick up Nicole. I'm not missing that party for anything.

JOHN: Oh! Did I tell you that Nicole called?

BRAD: She called? On my cell phone?

JOHN: Your phone was in the kitchen where I told you to leave it until the window was done.

BRAD: *(Starts OFF.)* I better call her back.

JOHN: Stop! *(BRAD stops and looks at him.)* You don't need to. I handled it.

BRAD: What do you mean? You talked to Nicole? What did she say? What did you say?

JOHN: She wanted to know what time you were picking her up tonight.

BRAD: What did you tell her?

JOHN: I told her the truth. Said you were busy with a few chores. That you couldn't make it and had to cancel.

BRAD: What the hell?!

JOHN: Oh, and I told her you'd be missing her surprise party at Milo's tonight.

BRAD: What?! You told her about the party? How could you do that?! You wouldn't believe what we've had to do to pull this off. Now you've ruined it for everyone! Why would you do this? Why?!

JOHN: (Shrugs and halfway smiles.) Thought she needed to know.

BRAD: You thought she needed to know?! How could you ruin it for her? She's never done anything to you!

JOHN: Not true. She distracts you from doing things around here. Look at that window. Still tons of streaks. Maybe you should try newspaper.

LUKE: We d-d-d-did.

JOHN: Well, maybe you should try using the shirts off your back. I don't care. Whatever it takes. Just get busy and do it. NOW! (EXITS as LUKE goes to the window and begins cleaning.)

BRAD: That's it! We're getting out of this hell hole!

LUKE: Wh-wh-wh-where are we g-g-g-going?

BRAD: I don't know. And I don't care. I'd rather live on the streets than in the same house with that bastard.

LUKE: You go. I'll st-st-st-stay here. I'll take care of M-M-Mom.

BRAD: I'm not leaving without you, Luke. Listen, it's you and me. Always has been.

LUKE: (Cleaning.) You g-g-g-go.

BRAD: No, we don't deserve this. You know that.

LUKE: You g-g-g-go.

BRAD: Did you hear what he just did? He's a bastard! Why? Because he can. That's his entire excuse for being an asshole. Because he can!

LUKE: I know. B-B-But Mom....

BRAD: Yeah, Mom, I know. But remember that time when we were like six and eight years old in the backseat of the car just giggling away?

LUKE: I r-r-r-remember.

BRAD: He said, "Shut up!" But we kept laughing. I don't remember why, but something was funny, and we just couldn't stop. And Dad kept yelling. "I said shut up!"

LUKE: He st-st-st-stopped the car.

BRAD: Yeah. He stopped the car, then he threw us out. We stopped laughing then, didn't we?

LUKE: We wa-wa-walked home. Took us all d-d-day.

BRAD: Yeah, then when we finally got home, he screamed at us to go straight to bed. No dinner for us. What a dad. What a dad! I'm done, Luke! I am so done. You've got to come with me!

LUKE: T-t-t-to to live on the st-st-st-streets?

BRAD: Maybe. Or maybe we'll stay at Jimmy's house for a few nights. We'll figure it out, Luke. I promise.

LUKE: O-k-k-k-kay.

BRAD: So here's the plan. We'll finish this window, and then when Dad thinks we're in the backyard pulling weeds, we'll grab some stuff out of our rooms, take whatever we need, throw it in my car, and get out of here. We're not coming back, Luke. You understand?

LUKE: Yes. N-n-n-not coming b-b-b-back. Not even for M-M-M-Mom.

BRAD: Let's finish this window. I'm ready to leave. *(They get the paper towels and glass cleaner and go back to washing the window.)*

SYNOPSIS: A bride-to-be is meeting with three of her bridesmaids to discuss dropping the fourth girl from her wedding party.

CAST: 5F
    Jade (mid-20s)
    Danielle (mid-20s)
    Gabriella (mid-20s)
    Maria (mid-20s)
    Allison (mid-20s)

SETTING: Any room
PROPS: None

MARIA is meeting with three of her bridesmaids—DANIELLE, GABRIELLA, and JADE—to discuss dropping the fourth girl, ALLISON, from her wedding party.

JADE: How are you going to tell her?

DANIELLE: Hasn't she already been fitted for her dress?

GABRIELLA: Tell her you're worried that the wedding will be too much for her.

DANIELLE: Tell her you're concerned about her health.

JADE: I don't get it. Why do you want to dump Allison as one of your bridesmaids?

GABRIELLA: Come on, Jade. You know, it's because of... well, you know.

JADE: I do?

DANIELLE: The big C? The diagnosis?

MARIA: I've been giving it a lot of thought.

JADE: So you don't want her in your wedding because she's been diagnosed with cancer?

MARIA: Can you blame me?

GABRIELLA: I totally get it, Maria. What if she's not feeling well on your wedding day? There you are with four groomsmen, but suddenly you only have three bridesmaids because she's not feeling well. Then what are you supposed to do? Grab some random girl off the street?

DANIELLE: And what about that wig she's wearing? It looks so unnatural for the wedding photos.

GABRIELLA: I say drop her now before it's too late.

MARIA: Exactly. *(To JADE.)* Danielle and Gabriella are right. This is supposed to be the happiest day of my life. Everything's supposed to be perfect. So I think it's fair that I don't want someone in my wedding party who has cancer.

JADE: Why not? It's not like it's contagious.

DANIELLE: Thank goodness! She was sitting next to me at the bridal shower and accidentally took a sip of my punch instead of hers. That freaked me out. I mean, I know it's not contagious or anything, but I couldn't drink my punch after that.

GABRIELLA: She's just so sickly to be around.

DANIELLE: Remember when Allison's hair was long?

MARIA: She had beautiful hair. And now that wig... ugh.

DANIELLE: I don't mean to sound rude, but it does look ugly.

GABRIELLA: You don't want that in your wedding pictures. Twenty years from now, when you're showing your teenage daughter your wedding photos, there will be that awful wig again.

DANIELLE: You need to replace her.

JADE: But Allison's been your friend since elementary school.

MARIA: I know that! But it's not my fault she has cancer.

JADE: It's not her fault, either!

DANIELLE: Jade, it's Maria's wedding. She gets to decide who she wants as her bridesmaids.

JADE: She already did, and she picked four of us. The two of you. Me. And Allison.

MARIA: I'll still be Allison's friend and support her any way I can. I mean, I pray that she gets better. Really, I do.

JADE: But three weeks before your wedding you're going to drop her as your bridesmaid?

MARIA: It sounds horrible when you say it like that, but yes. She needs to concentrate on getting well, not keeping up with us. It's too much for her.

GABRIELLA: Plus, she doesn't seem like herself. She seems depressed. Sad.

DANIELLE: Who needs that on their wedding day? It's supposed to be a happy occasion.

JADE: Maybe she's sad because the three of you are acting weird around her.

MARIA: No, we aren't.

JADE: Yes, you are. You act as if she's fragile and about to break.

DANIELLE: So? She is frail.

GABRIELLA: She's sick.

JADE: Oh, so she can't handle our crazy fun times? The jokes? The laughter? You three are the ones acting depressed when she's around.

MARIA: Well, cancer is depressing.

JADE: Don't do this. Allison has been one of our best friends forever. She'd be crushed if you eliminated her as one of your bridesmaids.

MARIA: My wedding is supposed to be perfect. This day is about me and Ricky. Not me and Allison. And I can't take the chance of her... you know.

JADE: What?

MARIA: Being sick on my wedding day.

JADE: She'll be fine. She's getting better every day.

MARIA: Better? The chemo is making her sick as a dog!

JADE: She'll have that all wrapped up soon. She'll be feeling just fine on the day you get married.

DANIELLE: You don't know that.

JADE: Yes, I do.

GABRIELLA: What if she faints at the wedding? Collapses. Then what? Stop the wedding to call an ambulance during the ceremony?

JADE: I know she's sick, but she says she's getting stronger every day, and I just know she's going to pull through this.

DANIELLE: You don't know that. Not for sure.

JADE: I know for sure that a positive attitude and encouragement from her closest friends will help her get through this.

MARIA: Like I said, I'm still going to be her friend.

GABRIELLA: So am I.

DANIELLE: Me too.

JADE: Friends, just not in your wedding. Because she has cancer.

MARIA: I think it will be too much for her.

JADE: Why don't you at least let her decide if it's too much?

DANIELLE: Why don't you support Maria in this and stop making her feel guilty?

GABRIELLA: I agree with Danielle. We should be supporting Maria. So what if she wants to replace one of her bridesmaids who is sick? It's her wedding.

JADE: So what? So what?! Do you want to know what I think?

DANIELLE: I think you've already told us.

GABRIELLA: More than once, I might add.

JADE: I think you three are the sick ones.

MARIA: Why would you say something so mean?

JADE: Because you plan to dump Allison as your bridesmaid at the last minute when you know how much she's looking forward to being a part of your wedding. It's one of those rare moments when she can feel normal and not sick. Those moments don't come along too often for her. But, no. You toss her out like garbage. So yes, I think you three are the sick ones.

GABRIELLA: That's not fair.

JADE: *(Looks at MARIA.)* What you're planning to do is mean.

DANIELLE: I disagree.

GABRIELLA: So do I.

JADE: And if you do this to Allison, then you can find two new bridesmaids, because I won't be a bridesmaid either.

MARIA: What? What are you saying?

GABRIELLA: I can't believe you're doing this!

DANIELLE: Grow up! This is not about you!

JADE: You're right. It's not about me. It's about doing the right thing.

MARIA: I'm still going to be her friend. Did you not hear me say that?

JADE: Like I said, you throw her out, then I'm out too.

ALLISON: *(ENTERS, smiling brightly.)* Hi! Am I late?

DANIELLE: Hey, Allison.

ALLISON: I'm sorry I'm late. I had a doctor's appointment, and he was running behind schedule.

JADE: How did your appointment go?

ALLISON: Good. Just one more round of chemo and I'm done. Thank goodness.

JADE: That's wonderful. Kick that cancer to the curb!

ALLISON: I hope so. I really hope so. I'm ready for things to get back to normal for me. *(Touches her wig.)* For my hair to grow back. To have more energy. And to be hungry again. I've lost twenty pounds. I just can't seem to find my appetite.

JADE: Well, you look great!

ALLISON: I do?

JADE: You do. Remember our saying?

ALLISON: *(Smiles.)* What doesn't kill us makes us stronger.

JADE: That's it! You're on a tough road, but you're nearing the finish line. Someday soon you'll look back and say, "Wow, I'm glad that's behind me!"

ALLISON: Yes, I will.

MARIA: Allison, there's something that I need to talk to you about.

DANIELLE: *(To MARIA.)* Do you want us to leave?

GABRIELLA: I think we should. Let's give them space to talk. *(She and DANIELLE EXIT.)*

ALLISON: What's going on?

JADE: Yeah, I'm leaving too. I refuse to be a part of this. *(Turns to ALLISON.)* Hey, I'll be right outside. I'll wait for you.

ALLISON: *(Confused.)* All right. *(To MARIA.)* What's going on, Maria?

JADE: One more thing before I go. *(To ALLISON.)* I want you to know I wholeheartedly disagree with Maria. And don't forget, I'll be outside waiting for you. *(EXITS.)*

ALLISON: What's going on?

MARIA: I, uh… need to talk to you about something.

ALLISON: My dress? You don't think it'll fit me anymore since I lost all that weight? I know. Me too. But don't worry because I was going to have the seamstress take it in a bit. You know, around the waist. Like this. *(Demonstrates.)*

It's such a pretty dress. I just love to twirl around in it. *(Twirls.)* Yellow is my favorite color. Bright and warm like sunshine. And feminine. It was such a great color choice. If I ever get married, I want my bridesmaids to wear yellow too. *(Smiles.)* And carry yellow and white daisies. I'm a copycat, aren't I? Oh, well. Don't worry because you'll be in my wedding too.

MARIA: I need to make some changes to my wedding.

ALLISON: Like what?

MARIA: Like... my bridesmaids.

ALLISON: What do you mean?

MARIA: I know you haven't been feeling well lately.

ALLISON: Oh, I'm feeling better every day. Like today, I managed to eat half of a hamburger. And that's huge for me. It's the most I've eaten in the past couple of months.

MARIA: I think it would be better if you weren't in my wedding. You know... so you can rest.

ALLISON: What?! You don't want me as a bridesmaid anymore?

MARIA: I thought you wouldn't feel up to it.

ALLISON: I will. I finish my last chemo session next week and then I'll start to feel stronger. That'll give me a good two weeks to get my energy level back before your wedding. I'll be okay. I promise.

MARIA: I'm sorry, but I don't want to take the chance.

ALLISON: You're dumping me?

MARIA: Not as a friend.

ALLISON: You're going to replace me?

MARIA: I already have. My cousin Monica is going to step in for you.

ALLISON: But I don't need someone to step in for me. I can still do it. Really, I can!

MARIA: Monica is thin like you. So, if you don't mind, can I have your dress so she can get fitted next week?

ALLISON: You want me to give her my dress? The dress I paid for with my own money? *(Sadly.)* The dress I like to... *(Slowly turns.)* ...twirl in?

MARIA: I'm sorry. It's just... you're not well. And don't worry. She'll pay you back for the dress.

ALLISON: But I thought you wanted your closest friends there with you on your wedding day.

MARIA: You can still come to the wedding.

ALLISON: Oh. Just not be in it. Right?

MARIA: I'm sorry.

ALLISON: *(Deep breath.)* All right. It's your wedding.

MARIA: Thank you for understanding.

ALLISON: I don't.

MARIA: I'm sorry.

ALLISON: Well, let's hope you never receive a bad report from your doctor. Let's hope you never become ill and have to go through the most difficult time in your entire life.

MARIA: I'm sorry.

ALLISON: And let's hope you never have to act strong when you're afraid. Or face the fear of dying.

MARIA: I can't even imagine...

ALLISON: But if you do ever have to go through any of this, I'll still be there for you. And you know what I'll tell you?

MARIA: What?

ALLISON: Look for the moments that help you forget.

MARIA: Forget?

ALLISON: The moments that help you forget you have cancer. Those rare moments when it slips your mind, and you actually laugh at a joke. Laugh till you cry. Or that moment when you look at yourself in the mirror and still believe you look beautiful, despite what's going on inside your body. Beautiful because you're wearing a pretty yellow dress. A pretty yellow dress that you catch yourself twirling around in as if you were a silly young girl. Or a princess in a fairytale. Or something wonderful like that. But be careful because those moments don't last. You look in the mirror and suddenly see an unfamiliar face with unfamiliar hair, or no hair, and you remember how cruel life can be. And how cruel people can be. And it hurts. It hurts so much. But then you think about that saying. "What doesn't kill us makes us stronger." So you smile, you push your shoulders back... *(She does this.)* ...and you wipe away your tears. *(Wipes a tear.)* And you remind yourself that you will overcome this. I will overcome this. *(Pause as she looks at*

MARIA.) Yes, let's hope you never know how much it hurts. *(Smiles.)* I sincerely hope you don't. *(As she turns to EXIT.)* I'll have the dress sent to your house later today. *(EXITS.)*

HER APPEARANCE

SYNOPSIS: A young woman talks with her deceased mother about the sadness in her life.

CAST: 2F
  Scarlet (24)
  Mom (51)

SETTING: Bedroom
PROPS: None

SCARLET stands alone in her bedroom as she speaks to her deceased mother.

SCARLET: Sometimes I wish you were here, Mom. Sometimes, you know, I pretend you are. What daughter doesn't need her mom? Maybe when I was thirteen, fourteen, or even fifteen, I thought I was too grown up for a mom. Too independent. Too smart. Too everything. But deep down inside I knew I still needed my mom. I especially know that now that you're gone. Sometimes I close my eyes and when I open them, you magically appear. I'm not sure how it happens, but it does. Oh, I know it's not real. But in my mind it is. And so what? My therapist says it's fine. Whatever helps. *(Closes her eyes and takes a deep breath.)*

MOM: *(ENTERS.)* What's wrong, Scarlet?

SCARLET: *(Opens her eyes and looks at MOM.)* Mom, you know what's wrong.

MOM: We can't undo what happened.

SCARLET: I know. That's why I just cry about it.

MOM: Crying doesn't change anything.

SCARLET: It did when I was seven.

MOM: You were being overly dramatic.

SCARLET: My tears got me Rascal.

MOM: Oh, I loved that dog! How is Rascal?

SCARLET: He's old, Mom. He doesn't chew up my shoes anymore. Or chase after his red ball. He sleeps a lot. I have him on pain medications. His arthritis gives him a lot of pain.

MOM: *(Smiles.)* Rascal was such a cute little puppy. That little bundle of brown curly fur. Those white ears. I'd say he's worth the tears.

SCARLET: So are you, Mom, if only it would bring you back.

MOM: It won't, so please don't cry about it anymore.

SCARLET: At least I can still pretend you're here.

MOM: I'm not sure it's healthy.

SCARLET: Oh, but it is. My therapist said it was all right.

MOM: You have a therapist?

SCARLET: Yes. I don't handle changes very well. Like death.

MOM: I'm sorry.

SCARLET: And there've been too many other changes lately. I told my therapist the only thing that could help me cope with everything was to have my mom around.

MOM: I'm here.

SCARLET: So...

MOM: So?

SCARLET: So, I have some news.

MOM: What's that?

SCARLET: Jake and I are calling it quits.

MOM: Oh, no. Why?

SCARLET: *(Shrugs.)* We grew apart.

MOM: I think there's more to it than that.

SCARLET: You're right. It's me. He wants to stay together, but I don't. Since we lost the baby... I don't feel the same.

MOM: About Jake?

SCARLET: About Jake. About my life.

MOM: You can't blame Jake for the loss of your baby.

SCARLET: I don't. I blame myself.

MOM: You can't blame yourself either. Accidents happen.

SCARLET: Believe me, Mom, I know. Remember when I was five? If it weren't for accidents, we'd still have Granny's vase on the coffee table. If it weren't for accidents, I wouldn't have this scar on my arm from when I was twelve. And if it weren't for accidents, I'd still have you in my life.

MOM: At least you can still pretend I'm in your life.

SCARLET: I'd rather have you here for real, Mom!

MOM: I'm here.

SCARLET: But only in my mind.

MOM: Maybe.

SCARLET: What do you mean, "maybe"?

MOM: Maybe I'm really here. Maybe you just think you're pretending I'm here when you need me, but maybe, just maybe, I really am here. Maybe I can sense that you need me, and I appear.

SCARLET: That's not possible.

MOM: Anything is possible. Didn't I teach you that?

SCARLET: Yes, but... it's me. I have issues. I'm taking anti-depressants, but I still feel sad most of the time.

MOM: Why are you so sad?

SCARLET: Why am I sad? I lost my mom, then my baby, and you're asking me that?

MOM: Yes, I am. Tell me why you're so sad, sweetie.

SCARLET: That's the question everyone asks. Jake, my friends, Dad, my therapist, you. It's such a simple question. But even if I had an answer, are there words of advice or comfort that will make this sadness go away? No. Perhaps a little white pill to do the trick? No. Counseling? Digging deeper into my soul and pulling out the culprits of my misery? Does it make me feel better? No. Am I hopeless? Yes. I'm a hopeless case, Mom.

MOM: No, you're not.

SCARLET: No?

MOM: No. You need to remember the things that I taught you. Life is too short—

SCARLET: Too short to complain?

MOM: Look at the bright side.

SCARLET: I can't see it.

MOM: Is the glass half full?

SCARLET: No, it's half empty. Empty without my baby. Without you.

MOM: Scarlet, that same glass is also half full. It's all in how you look at it. You are in charge of your own happiness.

SCARLET: Mind over matter?

MOM: And laughter is so important. Don't be afraid to laugh.

SCARLET: There's nothing to laugh about, Mom.

MOM: Oh, yes, there is. There was even something at my funeral.

SCARLET: Mom, what was funny? How could you say anything was funny at your funeral?

MOM: Because there was.

SCARLET: What?

MOM: When you showed up to my funeral wearing a pair of socks that didn't match.

SCARLET: You noticed?

MOM: *(Laughs.)* Yes. The socks were different colors. Not even close!

SCARLET: I guess that was kind of funny... in a sad sort of way.

MOM: It was funny! It was just like when you were three years old, and you'd put on my shoes and prance around the house. But you never had on a matching pair. A red shoe and a black shoe. A loafer and a sandal. It always made me laugh.

SCARLET: I don't remember.

MOM: I do. You were so adorable. That long wavy hair. Those dimples. You were spoiled rotten.

SCARLET: I was upset getting dressed for your funeral. I grabbed two socks out of my closet and never noticed they didn't match until I was looking at my feet during the service.

MOM: I noticed. *(Small laugh.)* I loved it.

SCARLET: You loved it?

MOM: Oh, come on! Admit it. It was funny.

SCARLET: *(Shrugs.)* It was sad if you ask me. Everything is sad to me, if you haven't noticed.

MOM: I've noticed.

SCARLET: When I was sitting in that pew listening to the pastor, I felt so numb. I couldn't even cry. I wanted to, but the tears wouldn't come. What I wanted to do was crawl into that casket with you. I wanted to hold onto you and die right there alongside you. Then they could close the casket, and we could escape together. But you left, and I'm stuck here without you.

MOM: I'm here, Scarlet.

SCARLET: No, you're not. You're just a figment of my imagination.

MOM: How do you know?

SCARLET: I know. You're not real.

MOM: Either way, real or not, I'm still your mom.

SCARLET: Will you be there when I wake up in the middle of the night and I can't go back to sleep again?

MOM: Yes.

SCARLET: When I walk through my new apartment and wonder where to hang the pictures? Will you be there then?

MOM: Yes.

SCARLET: When I feel sad and lonely and I want to call you? Will you be there?

MOM: Yes.

SCARLET: When I need advice?

MOM: Yes.

SCARLET: No, you won't! Got you on that one, Mom! You can't give me advice!

MOM: Why not?

SCARLET: Because you left me! You're not here. *(Taps her head.)* You're only in here. Which we both know is majorly messed up.

MOM: You think I left you?

SCARLET: Yes! You left, Mom!

MOM: Oh, honey. I didn't want to.

SCARLET: Whatever. You're still gone. Everyone who has ever meant anything to me is gone. Dad, he's buried himself in his work since you died. He can't deal with me and my problems. My baby. You. Rascal is almost gone too. And Jake... well, that's just a matter of time. Paperwork, actually. *(Holds out her arms.)* Hello, world. Here I am. Heartbroken, lonely, and distraught.

MOM: Enough!

SCARLET: What?

MOM: I said, enough already!

SCARLET: Are you yelling at me?

MOM: I've had enough of this!

SCARLET: Well, you should try living my life, then.

MOM: You need to adjust your attitude, young lady!

SCARLET: I can't.

MOM: I said, that's enough!

SCARLET: What are you going to do, Mom? Ground me? Send me to my room? Go ahead. I don't care. Actually, I don't care about anything anymore. Maybe...

MOM: Maybe what?

SCARLET: Maybe I should join you.

MOM: What do you mean?

SCARLET: I've thought about it.

MOM: What?

SCARLET: Joining you. Wherever it is you are.

MOM: What are you saying?

SCARLET: *(Smiles.)* We can walk through paradise together. We'll be together again, and everything will be better. My sadness will be gone. I will be there with you. Yes. That's what I should do. *(MOM slaps her face.)* Mom! *(Touches her face.)* Why did you do that?

MOM: I said, enough! Now you listen to me!

SCARLET: I can't believe you slapped me. And... and... I felt it.

MOM: I'm glad I got your attention.

SCARLET: You are here, aren't you, Mom?

MOM: I told you I was.

SCARLET: *(Falls into her arms.)* Oh, Mom!

MOM: Oh, Scarlet...

SCARLET: I want you back with me! I can't do this without you! Life is too hard. My heart has crumbled into a million pieces, and it'll never be whole again.

MOM: Listen to me, Scarlet.

SCARLET: I'm listening.

MOM: Good things are around the corner.

SCARLET: But I can't see them.

MOM: Patience. You and Jake are going to mend your relationship.

SCARLET: We are?

MOM: Yes, but it's up to you. You know Jake doesn't want to lose you.

SCARLET: I know. I know it's me. It's all me.

MOM: So go apologize to him. Talk to him. Tell him that you've decided to put the past where it belongs. Behind you. And that you're ready to move forward. And then there's the baby…

SCARLET: Mom, I can't get past that.

MOM: She's with me.

SCARLET: She's with you?

MOM: *(Smiles.)* Yes. So relax. It's all right.

SCARLET: Oh, Mom…

MOM: And you will have another baby soon.

SCARLET: How do you know?

MOM: I know.

SCARLET: Jake and I are going to have a baby?

MOM: Yes. Sooner than you think.

SCARLET: Are you sure? Are you really sure?

MOM: Yes. Would I lie to you?

SCARLET: No.

MOM: And you will teach her the things that I taught you. And you will let her wear your shoes. Mix-matched, of course.

SCARLET: *(Small laugh.)* Of course.

MOM: She'll parade through your home as you giggle at her clumsiness. And your heart will be so full and happy. *(Touches SCARLET'S face where she had slapped her earlier.)* No more sadness. And you will want all the happiness for your daughter that the world has to offer. As I do for you.

SCARLET: Oh, Mom…

MOM: So, like I said, enough is enough. Stop dwelling on the past. It's time to move forward.

SCARLET: You're right. You're always right.

MOM: That's better. Because life is grand. Full of new beginnings every day.

SCARLET: But it's also full of loss.

MOM: It's what makes the people we love so precious. Loss makes us love more deeply.

SCARLET: Love more deeply?

MOM: That's right.

SCARLET: I love you, Mom.

MOM: I love you too.

SCARLET: You're really here, aren't you?

MOM: Yes.

SCARLET: You've been here all along, haven't you?

MOM: I have. *(As she turns to leave.)* I love you. *(EXITS.)*

SCARLET: I love you too, Mom. *(Smiles.)* Okay, I think I can do this now.

THE RIOT

SYNOPSIS: An angry mother confronts her son, who participated in a race riot against police earlier that night.

CAST: 1M, 2F
   Tamika (14)
   Trevor (18)
   Mom (38)

SET: Apartment living room
PROPS: Couch, two cell phones

TREVOR is sprawled on the couch playing on his cell phone. His sister, TAMIKA, ENTERS.

TAMIKA: There you are. It's a good thing you're home.

TREVOR: *(Engaged in his game.)* What do you want, Tamika?

TAMIKA: It's not what I want. It's Mom. She called and she's on her way home to deal with you. Just thought you'd wanna know.

TREVOR: Deal with me? For what? What'd I do?

TAMIKA: I dunno. You tell me.

TREVOR: I didn't do nothin'.

TAMIKA: Yeah, right.

TREVOR: Mom never gets home before two in the morning. She leavin' early?

TAMIKA: Yeah. She called a while ago. I told her I hadn't seen you. Then she started yelling. "If you see your brother, you tell him to stay there and not leave!" So you heard it. Stay here and don't leave. What'd you do this time, Trevor?

TREVOR: Nothin'.

TAMIKA: Right. Well, you better hurry and come up with a good excuse 'cause you're in big trouble with Mom. And I mean like never before.

TREVOR: She won't do nothin' but holler for a while.

TAMIKA: I wouldn't count on that. Boy, you must've done something really bad this time.

TREVOR: *(Stands and paces.)* Not really. But I wonder how she found out. How much she knows.

TAMIKA: *(Checks the time on her cell phone.)* Well, you're about to find out. She'll be home any minute now. Hey, you need an alibi? *(Holds out hand.)* I accept cash.

TREVOR: Go away.

TAMIKA: Come on, tell your little sister what kinda trouble you got into this time. You and Bobby skip school again?

TREVOR: No.

TAMIKA: Oh, I know! I bet someone told Mom they saw you walkin' 'cross the tracks with one of them stupid cigarillos hangin' outta your mouth. Uh-huh. She's gonna bust you good for that.

TREVOR: Mom wouldn't leave her night job over me havin' one cigarillo.

TAMIKA: Wanna bet?

TREVOR: I wasn't smoking. Not today at least.

TAMIKA: Then what'd ya do?

TREVOR: *(Shakes his head.)* Nothin' bad.

TAMIKA: You want some advice?

TREVOR: No.

TAMIKA: *(Ignores him.)* Here's what I suggest. You need to practice your so-called excuse on me. That way I can tell you if it sounds good. If not, well, my offer still stands for being your alibi. Like I said, cash works.

TREVOR: Go away, Tamika.

TAMIKA: You don't have much time. So, go ahead. Let me hear your best excuse. Better make it good.

TREVOR: I wish I had a clue how much Mom knows.

TAMIKA: Count on everything and pray for little. But until you know for sure, admit to nothin'.

TREVOR: I'll admit to everything!

TAMIKA: Whoa! You sure you don't wanna re-think that?

TREVOR: No. And for the record, I'm not sorry either!

TAMIKA: Double whoa! When Mom hears that, you are goin' down. And I mean DOWN. D-O-W-N! You know, you could try actin' a bit remorseful.

TREVOR: Mom won't get it. But I'm not sorry.

TAMIKA: You will be. When Mom's finished with you, believe me, you'll be sorry. I've never heard her so pissed.

TREVOR: Whatever.

TAMIKA: Oh, and my last bit of advice for you is this. Let Mom do all the talkin'. Let her yell, threaten, and promise to ruin your life. If you're smart, you'll say nothin'. And always agree. Agree she's right and you was wrong. That is, if you want to see the light of day again. *(Shakes head.)* You're always causin' Mom so much trouble. You know, she's doing the best she can. Workin' two jobs, bein' both our mom and dad.

TREVOR: I'm glad Dad's not around.

TAMIKA: Since when?

TREVOR: Since always.

TAMIKA: That's not true, and you know it! When you was a kid you was always cryin' for him.

TREVOR: I hardly even remember him now. But the stuff I do remember ain't good.

TAMIKA: I sorta remember. I remember him yellin'. And Mom cryin'. I'm glad he's gone.

TREVOR: Me too.

TAMIKA: If he'd been a better dad—

TREVOR: He wasn't.

TAMIKA: I'm just sayin'... if he had been a better person, you'd want him to be around. So would I.

TREVOR: Well, he's not. Last Mom heard, he was in prison. Don't know for what. I hope he never gets out.

TAMIKA: Yeah, me too. I mean, I don't figure he'd ever get out and wanna come back here and get to know us. Do you?

TREVOR: No.

TAMIKA: You know, just to see how we turned out. See if his daughter—probably doesn't even remember my name—made something of herself, or... or followed in his pathetic footsteps.

TREVOR: Neither one of us will turn out like him. Ever.

TAMIKA: That's why Mom comes down on you so hard. She doesn't want you to turn out like Dad.

MOM: *(ENTERS.)* There you are!

TAMIKA: Mom, what's wrong? Why are you mad at Trevor?

MOM: Tamika, go to your room. I need to speak to your brother. Alone.

TAMIKA: But I wanna hear—

MOM: Now!

TAMIKA: Okay, okay. *(To TREVOR.)* Remember what I told you. *(Leans in.)* And say you're sorry. *(EXITS.)*

MOM: Well?

TREVOR: What's up?

MOM: What's up? Seriously?

TREVOR: Yeah. What are you so mad about?

MOM: Mad doesn't even begin to cover it. Do you have any idea how disappointed I am in you right now? Do you?

TREVOR: No, I don't even know what you're talkin' about.

MOM: I do my best to raise my kids right and where does it get me? I teach you right from wrong. I take you to church. I give you everything you need without spoiling you. I provide you the best home possible. Oh, I know it's not much, but we get by. And where does all this get me? Huh? Where does this get me, Trevor? *(Silence.)* Say something! *(More silence.)* I said, say something!

TREVOR: What do you want me to say?

MOM: I want you to tell me what you were doing tonight at that riot.

TREVOR: Who told you?

MOM: I got a call from Mrs. Evans. Seems you made tonight's ten o'clock news. She said they got a real good close-up of you.

TREVOR: You want me to say I'm sorry? Because I'm not. We had every right to be there tonight.

MOM: You had no right!

TREVOR: Yes, we did. We need to be heard. Our voices matter!

MOM: Violence is how you try to be heard?

TREVOR: Yeah, Mom! Come on! You know they arrested Jamal because of the color of his skin.

MOM: Jamal was arrested because the police believe he killed someone.

TREVOR: He didn't do it!

MOM: How do you know? Were you there when that poor woman was murdered?

TREVOR: No, 'course not. But I know he didn't do it! He's Jay's brother. And Jay's brother would never do nothin' like that.

MOM: You don't know everything, Trevor. Let the police do their investigation.

TREVOR: He'll get framed. They just need someone to hang it on.

MOM: He won't get framed. The truth will come out.

TREVOR: Well, I know Jamal didn't do it.

MOM: This isn't about what Jamal did. This is about what you did.

TREVOR: What?

MOM: Don't you "What?" me! Every news station in the area had their cameras on the riot. And what did everyone see while I was mopping floors at the bakery? You! Mrs. Evans and the entire city saw my son throwing a brick through a store window while other people were inside stealing stuff and destroying property!

TREVOR: So what?! The cops are tryin' to destroy Jamal's life!

MOM: They arrested him for destroying somebody else's life!

TREVOR: But he didn't do it! I'll tell you why he was arrested. Because he has the wrong color skin!

MOM: Maybe that's true, Trevor, and it's wrong. But let me set you straight, Trevor Dale Lewis. Two wrongs do not make a right! They never do! Ever! Do you hear me? Because when you get angry and lash out, you are no better than the injustice you are angry about.

TREVOR: You're wrong! They need to listen to us!

MOM: Who? Who needs to listen to you?

TREVOR: Everyone! Especially the cops! We need to be heard! Things aren't right!

MOM: The police can't listen to you. They're too busy protecting law-abiding citizens from your destructive behavior!

TREVOR: They can't be allowed to just go around pointin' their fingers at folks who ain't their same skin color.

MOM: You listen here, young man! Your actions were not justified! Destroying someone else's property is never justified!

TREVOR: Why not? We're protestin'! We're gettin' their attention! Maybe it's the only way to get their attention. Because otherwise they don't listen to us.

MOM: Protesting is fine if it's done in a civilized manner. Holding signs, writing letters, speaking up. That's all fine. But throwing bricks through windows is never acceptable!

TREVOR: *(Shrugs.)* It got their attention.

MOM: You think that destroying the property of hard-working business owners and then looting their goods is okay if it gets attention? The poor family that owns that store has nothing to do with Jamal.

TREVOR: So?

MOM: So?! All it showed was disrespect, anger, and violence. None of these things are right, no matter what color your skin is. No matter what's not right in the world. It just makes all of us look bad.

TREVOR: It showed them that we mean business! That our voices matter!

MOM: Your actions matter too! Didn't I teach you that? Oh, where did I go wrong with you?

TREVOR: Jamal shouldn't have been arrested, and you know that.

MOM: I don't know that, and neither do you. I don't know all the facts. You don't know all the facts. You're just running on emotions.

TREVOR: Of course I am. Things need to change!

MOM: And you think what you did tonight will change things? If anything, it will only make things worse.

TREVOR: Maybe for now. But things gotta get better.

MOM: Trevor, believe it or not, I agree with you on that. But tonight only proves one thing.

TREVOR: What?

MOM: That you and your friends are out of control. Just like the person who murdered that woman, God rest her soul. Whether it was Jamal or not, that's for the police to investigate. But your actions disgrace yourself, our family, this city... and might I add, our race!

TREVOR: But it's not right that he was arrested!

MOM: What if he's guilty?

TREVOR: He's not.

MOM: What if the police have evidence that proves he is?

TREVOR: They don't.

MOM: You don't know that. What if he is?

TREVOR: He's not!

MOM: Listen to me! For the sake of discussion, what if he's guilty?

TREVOR: What if Jamal is guilty?

MOM: Yes.

TREVOR: *(Shrugs.)* Then he should go to prison.

MOM: So in that case, what have your actions proven? Anything?

TREVOR: I don't know. Maybe.

MOM: And let's say he's innocent.

TREVOR: He is.

MOM: Again, what have your actions proven?

TREVOR: That I'm angry. That judgin' someone based on their skin color is wrong!

MOM: I see. What if, Trevor… what if your father were still around?

TREVOR: He's not. Don't go there, Mom.

MOM: But let's say he was. Remember how he beat the living daylights out of me, but no one ever saw him do it? They had no way of knowing the truth.

TREVOR: You could've told them.

MOM: I suppose I could've. God knows maybe I should have. But what if they didn't believe me? Because after all, especially on the outside, your father seemed like such a nice guy.

TREVOR: Yeah, he was good at faking that.

MOM: Or let's say the police did believe me and maybe they had evidence to prove that your father had beat me, so they arrested him.

TREVOR: Good!

MOM: But your father was screaming, "It's a lie! I didn't do it! I'd never hurt my wife!" Sound like something he'd say?

TREVOR: Yeah, so?

MOM: So let's say your father's friends were furious he was arrested. They believed him. Not me. Not the evidence.

TREVOR: What's your point, Mom?

MOM: So let's just say they thought it was unfair.

TREVOR: Okay, okay. I see where you're goin' with this. But it's not the same.

MOM: His friends were so mad they broke all the windows at Patterson's Grocery.

TREVOR: Maybe they needed to express themselves. Tell the cops they're wrong.

MOM: And while they're at it, they spray painted the walls and made a real mess of everything.

TREVOR: Mr. Patterson probably has insurance for stuff like that.

MOM: Sure, but how would you feel about seeing our grocery store ruined like that? You know how hard Mr. Patterson works to keep the place nice. So do you still say who cares? No big deal? It's their right? Broken glass. Knocked over shelves. Busted everything. So, Trevor, how would that reveal the truth?

TREVOR: I don't know.

MOM: The truth is right here on my body. The scars. The bruises. The broken bones. It's my truth, not theirs. And your father... he was guilty all along.

TREVOR: I know, Mom.

MOM: Trevor, violence over the fear of injustice is just that. Violence. No matter how you look at it, it's wrong. Got it?

TREVOR: *(Nods.)* Got it.

MOM: It makes our entire race look bad. You know there will be consequences.

TREVOR: I'm in big trouble, aren't I?

MOM: Yes, you are, son. But not by me.

TREVOR: What do you mean?

MOM: The police are saying they'll arrest the people who were causing trouble tonight. They have it all on tape from the news stations. And what will your defense be? That you wanted to be heard? They heard you all right. But not the message you wanted to send.

TREVOR: I'm sorry, Mom. I really am. I'm just so mad. It doesn't seem right what they're doing to Jamal, and I want to be heard. *(Pause.)* What do I do now?

137

MOM: I honestly don't know. But believe it or not, I know exactly how you feel. I know how it feels to not be heard. *(TREVOR hugs her.)*

⟫ THE FOUNTAIN ⟫

SYNOPSIS: A lonely young woman questions why people bother making wishes.

CAST: Flexible cast of 4-7 (written as 1M, 6F, but can be 0-3M, 4-7F, doubling possible)
>   Sue (mid-40s)
>   Katie (20s)
>   Isabel* (30s)
>   Rachel (20s)
>   Andy* (18)
>   Haley (20s)
>   Francis* (70s)

*Gender flexible. Character names can change to ISAAC, ANDI, and FRANCES, as needed, with no line changes necessary.

SETTING: In front of the fountain at a large, indoor mall
PROPS: Bench, shopping bags

KATIE sits on a bench in front of a fountain at the local mall. SUE, disheveled and dressed sloppily, ENTERS carrying several shopping bags.

SUE: *(Plops down next to KATIE.)* Oh, this is my favorite place to sit down and rest. Right here in front of this beautiful fountain. It's so mesmerizing how the water shoots up then cascades down, don't you think?

KATIE: It's curious.

SUE: Why do you say that?

KATIE: Full of coins. Holding the wishes of people who pass by. Do you do that? Toss a coin into the fountain and hope your wish comes true?

SUE: No. I don't believe in all that. *(Small laugh.)* But I do believe in knowing who I'm talking with. *(Offers her hand.)* I'm Sue.

KATIE: *(Shakes her hand.)* Hi, Sue. I'm Katie.

SUE: Nice to meet you, Katie. Now to give my feet a quick rest. *(Looks around.)* Don't you just love people watching?

KATIE: It is interesting.

SUE: The mall is the best place for that.

KATIE: Yes. Detach yourself from society and observe.

SUE: You know, you can tell a lot about a person by the way they dress.

KATIE: You think so?

SUE: I do. For instance, *(Points.)* that woman over there wearing that yellow and black polka dotted dress. It's dizzy. But I bet you anything she has a bold personality, don't you think?

KATIE: Probably so. You'd have to be confident to wear a dress like that.

SUE: *(Points.)* And that woman over there in the blue pantsuit. I can tell you that she's a very serious individual. Her motto is, "Let's skip the chit-chat and get right down to the nitty-gritty."

KATIE: You're very good at this.

SUE: *(Points.)* Look at that woman. Now, she speaks perfection. Not a strand of hair out of place. *(Pause.)* I wonder what people think of me? *(Nudges KATIE and laughs.)* Maybe they think I just rolled out of bed. *(Nudges her again and giggles.)* Well, I practically did.

KATIE: *(Pause. She takes a deep breath.)* I just look at people and wonder.

SUE: What do you wonder?

KATIE: I wonder what it would be like to be them.

SUE: *(Chuckles.)* Well, I look at some of their wardrobe choices, and I'm glad that I'm me. Sloppy or not. *(Points.)* Look at that. That red and orange thingy isn't working for me. Is it working for you?

KATIE: I wonder if she's happy?

SUE: Well, she dresses happy, that's for sure.

KATIE: Yeah. *(Takes a deep breath.)* Sometimes I wish I could be someone else. *(Points.)* Like her. Colorful, vibrant, confident. *(Pause.)* Happy.

SUE: Aren't you happy? *(KATIE shrugs. SUE pats her leg.)* Life's too short not to be happy. You just have to put your mind to it. *(Stands.)* Well, I'm off. Off to find more sales. It's the only way I shop. Have a great day, Katie! Be happy!

KATIE: Thanks, you too. *(SUE EXITS.)*

ISABEL: *(Stops in front of KATIE to look at the water fountain. Speaks to herself.)* It's been years, but... why not? *(Reaches into her pocket for a coin and holds it up. [NOTE: all coins should be mimed.])* I wish... Let me see... what do I wish? *(She does not hear KATIE as she speaks behind her.)*

KATIE: Make it count.

ISABEL: I wish... I wish for a hugely successful party tonight.

KATIE: I want to come to your party.

ISABEL: If everything goes right, there will be impressions made, visions heard, and contracts signed.

KATIE: I'm impressed. I'd sign.

ISABEL: Million-dollar deal... *(Tosses the coin.)* Here's to you! *(Smiles brightly to KATIE.)* I don't know if I'll get my wish, but it doesn't hurt to try. I love my life! *(EXITS.)*

RACHEL: *(ENTERS, looking at the fountain. Pulls out a coin. Sighs.)* Here's to love. And to happily ever after. *(Tosses the coin.)*

KATIE: That's a good wish.

RACHEL: *(RACHEL looks back at KATIE.)* I'm getting married next week.

KATIE: Congratulations.

RACHEL: I've never been so happy!

KATIE: I've never been so sad.

RACHEL: What did you say?

KATIE: I hope you and your fiancé are very happy together.

RACHEL: Oh, thank you. I still have so much to do. *(Looks at watch.)* Oh, I better get going.

KATIE: Wait! Do you believe that wishes come true?

RACHEL: From tossing coins into a fountain?

KATIE: Yes.

RACHEL: *(Smiles.)* Oh, yeah! Why not? It's too bad everyone doesn't believe. It can't hurt.

KATIE: I think people hope their wishes come true, but they don't necessarily believe they will.

RACHEL: Well, you have to believe. Then maybe they will come true. *(Looks at her.)* Sorry, but like I said, I need to go now. So much to do! *(EXITS. After a moment, ANDY ENTERS.)*

ANDY: *(Tosses a coin into the fountain.)* I wish to win the lottery.

KATIE: Do you believe?

ANDY: *(Turns.)* What?

KATIE: Do you believe your wish will come true?

ANDY: *(Snaps.)* I don't know! I hope it does.

KATIE: A lot of people wish for the same thing.

ANDY: So?

KATIE: So, do you believe it'll happen?

ANDY: I don't know, maybe.

KATIE: Because wishes are just wishes. And coins tossed into a fountain don't seal the wish or make it come true.

ANDY: *(Digs into his pocket to find another coin.)* I wish negative people out of my life. *(Tosses the coin. Turns to KATIE and gives her a dirty look.)*

KATIE: You know, if you really want to win the lottery…

ANDY: What?

KATIE: You have to believe. At least that's what I've heard.

ANDY: Fine! *(Takes another coin from his pocket.)* I believe I'll win the lottery! *(Tosses the coin.)*

KATIE: Good luck.

ANDY: Luck?

KATIE: Yes.

ANDY: You just said it was about believing. Not about having luck.

KATIE: Then may your wish come true.

ANDY: *(Shakes his head.)* Weirdo. *(EXITS.)*

HALEY: *(ENTERS and goes to the fountain.)* I need to make a wish!

KATIE: Good luck.

HALEY: *(Turns.)* What?

KATIE: Nothing.

HALEY: *(Back to the fountain.)* I wish for peace, joy, and happiness for all mankind. *(Tosses a coin.)*

KATIE: That's impossible.

HALEY: *(Turns to KATIE.)* Did you say something?

KATIE: What you wished for can't happen.

HALEY: Huh?

KATIE: Peace, joy, and happiness for all mankind? It's not possible.

HALEY: Yes, it is. If you believe.

KATIE: How?

HALEY: By creating it. With a smile, a kind word...

KATIE: I'd take that.

HALEY: What?

KATIE: A smile. A kind word.

HALEY: *(Sits by KATIE.)* Do you come here often?

KATIE: Yeah, I work here at the mall. I often sit here on my lunch break. I watch as people are drawn to this—what seems to be, in their minds—magical fountain. As if it holds the power to grant wishes. Everyone is so happy to toss their coins in, from kids to elderly people.

HALEY: What do you suppose the older people wish for?

KATIE: I often wonder that myself. Perhaps to go back in time.

HALEY: Which is impossible.

KATIE: But if you wish...

FRANCIS: *(ENTERS and stands in front of fountain.)* I wish... *(Stops speaking, then tosses a coin into the fountain.)*

HALEY: What did you wish for?

FRANCIS: *(Turns to the YOUNG WOMEN.)* Oh, but I'm not supposed to tell!

HALEY: That's when you blow out birthday candles, not for coins in a fountain. Please?

FRANCIS: Well, I suppose, since it can't come true anyway. I wished that I could go back in time.

KATIE: *(To HALEY.)* Told you.

FRANCIS: At least go back to my childhood home just one more time. I wish I could sit on that porch and embrace every wonderful memory. Mama hanging clothes on the line. Papa fiddling in his workshop. Sara and Millie catching fireflies.

HALEY: You should go back.

FRANCIS: It's far away from here. But maybe... *(Holds up another coin.)* Maybe someday I will find my way back there. *(Tosses the coin.)* I wish.

KATIE: You have to believe.

FRANCIS: Yes. And never stop believing. *(EXITS.)*

KATIE: That's it!

HALEY: What?

KATIE: What the fountain represents. Dreams, hopes, desires. That's what I've been missing.

HALEY: What do you mean?

KATIE: Maybe the wishes don't come true.

HALEY: But maybe they do.

KATIE: But it's the hope that maybe, just maybe, their wish will come true. That hope ignites all the excitement. It's all about the hope.

HALEY: Have you ever thrown a coin into the fountain?

KATIE: No. Never.

HALEY: Never? After all the time you've sat here watching others? You've never done it yourself?

KATIE: I just feel sorry for them. Maybe even jealous.

HALEY: Jealous. Why?

KATIE: Because they're so happy. They have hope believing that their wishes can come true. I want to be like them with all their eagerness, and yet, I thought it was a lie. But now I understand better. It's not that the fountain grants your wishes, it's that the fountain gives you a moment to stop and hope. To hope for something good.

HALEY: Exactly. To visualize something positive.

KATIE: I've been so lonely. I'm new in town, and I have a new job here. But my family's in a different state, and I'm all alone. So, I come to this fountain and watch people throw coins into it and make wishes, even though I always believed it was pointless.

HALEY: *(Hands her a coin.)* Your turn.

KATIE: Should I?

HALEY: Yes, you should.

KATIE: *(Stands, steps forward, and closes her eyes. After a moment, she opens her eyes and tosses the coin into the fountain. Smiles.)* I did it.

HALEY: What did you wish for?

KATIE: Oh, I'm not telling!

HALEY: Well, whatever it is, I hope it comes true.

KATIE: Me too, thanks.

HALEY: By the way, my name is Haley.

KATIE: I'm Katie.

HALEY: Hey, do you want to catch a movie with me after you get off work? I hate going to the movies alone, don't you?

KATIE: Sure! I get off work at four, if you don't mind waiting till then.

HALEY: That's perfect! I can finish my shopping and grab some food and then meet you back here. Do you like scary movies? That's what I was planning on seeing.

KATIE: I love them!

HALEY: Great! It'll be fun. I usually get a big bucket of popcorn, so I'm happy to share.

KATIE: With lots of butter, I hope.

HALEY: Oh, yes! Lots of butter. Okay, I'll meet you back here at four.

KATIE: Sounds great! *(HALEY EXITS. KATIE goes to the fountain and smiles.)* What do you know? My wish has already come true. Thank you.

➤➤WHAT YOU SEE IS WHAT YOU GET➤➤

SYNOPSIS: Intertwined monologues delivered by a young woman and her mother reveal their different perspectives on the young woman's sexual preference.

CAST: (2F)
  Jasmine (early 20s)
  Mom (40s)

SETTING: None
PROPS: Ball cap

JASMINE wears baggy jeans, a men's shirt, and a ball cap turned backwards. MOM wears a conservative dress. Each character delivers her monologue to the audience as if confiding in a friend. They do not interact with each other.

MOM: I always put my daughter in pretty little dresses with matching bows. Pink. Especially pink.

JASMINE: I never liked dresses and bows.

MOM: But in middle school, everything changed. That's when she started acting like... a boy.

JASMINE: Mom never understood where I was coming from. I think she tried, but only from the viewpoint that if she could understand me, then she could change me. I'd tell her, "Mom, quit trying to turn me into some prissy little girl, because it's not going to happen."

MOM: At first I thought she was just going through a phase. You know, a tomboy phase. I thought surely it would pass.

JASMINE: *(Pulls on her ball cap.)* I'm not changing for anyone. What you see is what you get.

MOM: But after a while, I really became concerned. She didn't seem to like boys.

JASMINE: I have plenty of guy friends, but that's all they are— friends.

MOM: Gently—very gently—I encouraged her to like this boy named Carl. He was in the youth group at church. So nice.

And good looking too. I told her, "If I were your age, that's the boy I'd have a crush on."

JASMINE: Once Mom tried to push me towards this boy at church. It wasn't a pretty sight.

MOM: One day, I suggested she ask Carl to the Sadie Hawkins dance. You know, that dance where the girls ask the boys. I even talked to Carl's mom to make sure he wasn't already going with somebody else. Well, you should have seen my daughter's reaction.

JASMINE: You could call it a slight explosion. *(Yells.)* "Stop it! Stop telling me what to do!"

MOM: You'd think I had suggested she sign up for Girl Scouts. Well, I did that too, but that was a different fit of its own.

JASMINE: "Why do you do this?! Why do you always try to force me to do something that I don't want to do? How would you like it? Huh? How would you like it?" *(With a sudden thought.)* "And you already talked to his mom? The two of you set this up? This is so embarrassing! I will never forgive you! Do you hear me? I will never forgive you! I'm not asking him to that stupid dance! I hate him! And I hate you too!"

MOM: Believe me, she made sure I was sorry I ever suggested the dance with Carl.

JASMINE: Carl was nice enough, but he wasn't really my type, if you know what I mean.

MOM: She's not at all interested in going out with boys.

JASMINE: Now, if Carl was named "Carla," then I might have been interested in going to the dance.

MOM: If only I could put my finger on what caused her to turn out like this.

JASMINE: You could say I've been like this forever. As a kid, I didn't like Barbie dolls or pink. I'd much rather play with toy trucks or catch spiders in the yard. It's just who I was, but Mom thought she could change me.

MOM: She never did exhibit any feminine qualities. Not in any way. Believe me, I tried to steer her toward feminine things. Like when she was a little girl, I would paint her fingernails pink. But she would glare at her nails and scrape off every bit of the polish.

JASMINE: Like, she would paint my fingernails, and I hated it. I like fingernail polish now... *(Smiles.)* ...if it's black.

MOM: Bottom line is...

JASMINE: Bottom line is... she's embarrassed.

MOM: ...I'm embarrassed. I have a beautiful daughter who dresses and acts like a boy.

JASMINE: Embarrassed that I like baggy jeans, flannel shirts, and short hair. So what?

MOM: I mean, it's hard for me to admit this, but... I'm ashamed to call her my daughter.

JASMINE: Who's ashamed of their own child? My mom, that's who.

MOM: I want a daughter I can be friends with. Every so often have one of those mother-daughter days. You know, get pedicures, go shopping, giggle about our celebrity crushes.

JASMINE: She wanted a daughter who was a girly girl. But that's not what she got, is it?

MOM: *(Smiles.)* I've always loved her name. Jasmine Marie. Isn't that a pretty name?

JASMINE: *(Pulls on her ball cap.)* Even though my name's Jasmine, that's not what most people call me.

MOM: But that's not what most people call her. At least under their breath.

JASMINE: You know what they call girls like me.

MOM: You know what they call girls like her.

JASMINE: But I don't care.

MOM: But she doesn't care. At least that's what she says.

JASMINE: Yeah... I get called a lot of names. Lesbo. Dyke. Butch. Just to name a few.

MOM: I believe there are two different kinds of people in the world. You're either one or the other. A man or a woman. If you're born a man, then you should act like a man. If you're born a woman, then you should act like a woman.

JASMINE: Whatever. *(Pulls on her ball cap.)* Like I said, what you see is what you get.

MOM: I used to wonder if my daughter could've been switched at birth. Maybe I almost wished she had been. Does that make me a horrible person?

JASMINE: My mom thinks I'm horrible.

MOM: Not that she's horrible. After all, she does have some wonderful qualities.

JASMINE: I wonder if my mom could even say two or three nice things about me.

MOM: Like puzzles! She's very good at putting jigsaw puzzles together. Dump a thousand pieces on the table, and she will work on it for hours on end. Then a few days later, you walk into the room and what was once a pile of little cardboard pieces is now a beautiful lighthouse on the shore. You know, not everyone has such patience.

JASMINE: She couldn't say patience is one of my virtues. You get in my face, I'll get right back in yours. *(Steps forward.)* "You want to mess with me? Huh? Do you?"

MOM: And something else. She doesn't smoke.

JASMINE: And I smoke. Mom would be heartbroken if she knew this. So I sneak my cigarettes and use mouthwash. I mean, why give her one more reason to be disappointed in me?

MOM: And no tattoos! Thank goodness she doesn't have a tattoo.

JASMINE: Here's another thing she doesn't know... I have three tattoos. All hidden of course. Seems like I hide a lot of things from my mom, huh? Anyway, there's a peace sign. *(Points somewhere on her body.)* It's right here. And a cross... *(Points.)* ...right here. And last but not least... right here... *(Points.)* ...a lighthouse. I like lighthouses. Maybe it's from all those jigsaw puzzles I used to put together. I'm thinking about getting another tattoo. I want to get an American flag. For freedom. Yeah. *(Indicates her wrist.)* I'd like to put that one right here. Of course, my mom would see it then. *(Shrugs.)* But it's an expression of freedom. That I'm free to be myself.

MOM: See? That's three good things about her. *(Pause.)* So, here's what I think happened.

JASMINE: My mom's always looking for an excuse for me. A reason. Something to put her finger on.

MOM: She needed a father.

JASMINE: My mom blames my lack of having a father for, as she says, my behavior. Yes, *(Air quotes.)* "my behavior." It sounds like I have some sort of mental illness, doesn't it?

As if I could just take a daily pill to correct my shameful, unmentionable actions.

MOM: She needed that male influence in her life.

JASMINE: In my mom's world, it's the absent father's fault. "Oh, father, where art thou?"

MOM: So to compensate... well, you know.

JASMINE: My parents divorced when I was three. My father was rarely around. Mom would like to blame that, but... *(Shakes head.)* She's just looking for an excuse.

MOM: If it's not that, then...

JASMINE: To her, the only other possible explanation for me shunning any and all aspects of femininity is her worst nightmare.

MOM: ...then it's me. Yes, me. My fault. I mean, what if my over-the-top expectations for lady-like behavior caused this? Demanding she wear those frilly dresses even when she rebelled, forcing her to sleep in curlers, insisting on tea parties and ballet classes? Ignoring her love of trucks and dinosaurs, only to buy her one more pink dress? What if I caused this?

JASMINE: But the truth of the matter is...

MOM: So, yes, I blame myself.

JASMINE: ...it's nobody's fault. I found my way here all by myself. It's called being me. How simple a statement is that? Being me. Find yourself and be yourself. Rocket science? I don't think so. I like girls. That's all there is to it.

MOM: And in all honesty...

JASMINE: It's like, "Can we all be honest here?"

MOM: ...I'm heartbroken.

JASMINE: Or what if we all sang that Barney song? *(Or change to a current preschool character that teaches acceptance.)* Something about you loving me and me loving you and in the end, we're a happy family? Isn't that what Barney taught us? So why didn't we all grow up to be more open-minded? Didn't we all watch Barney?

MOM: If only I knew for sure what caused her to turn out like she did. Her lack of a father figure... or me?

JASMINE: I know my mom is thinking, "If only I could change her." But she can't.

MOM: If only I could change her. If only... if only there was a magic button, a re-do, an undo, or a backspace key. Does that make me a terrible mother?

JASMINE: Now I'm not saying she's a terrible mother. I could easily say three nice things about her. You bet I could. One. She keeps a nice house. I don't especially like clutter, and she's good at organization and tidiness. Two. She's a friendly person. Everyone who comes in contact with her leaves feeling better about themselves. And she smiles at people and hugs them. She even looks into their eyes and truly listens. *(Shrugs.)* Well, except to me. So there's two. Three. She can be a lot of fun. At least... at least she used to be a lot of fun.

MOM: I didn't start out terrible. *(Laughs.)* Oh, I remember this time when she was five or six years old, and we went to the county fair.

JASMINE: What mom would throw a hundred rings at soda bottles to win her kid a goldfish? My mom, that's who.

MOM: She wanted a goldfish, and I was determined to win her one. "Ten rings for five dollars? Sure, I can do this." *(As if tossing a ring.)* "Come on! Come on! Get on there!" *(Looks down as if talking to a younger Jasmine.)* "Watch this! I'm going to make it this time!" *(Leans forward, tosses another ring.)* "Missed again?" *(As if speaking to the carnival person.)* "Give me ten more rings." *(To a younger Jasmine.)* "I'm going to do it this time. I know! Maybe if I do something crazy."

JASMINE: *(Laughs.)* She was crazy.

MOM: "Watch this! I'm going to turn my back, close my eyes, and land this silly ring on that bottle!" *(Turns around, closes her eyes, and tosses.)* "There!" *(Pause.)* "What? I did it?" *(Turns back around.)* "I really did it?" *(Laughing.)* "Look at that! Your mother just won you a goldfish! Did you see that?"

JASMINE: When I was a little kid, we went to this fair. Fifty dollars later, I was carrying around a goldfish in a plastic bag. I was so happy.

MOM: *(Looking down.)* "What are you going to name him?"

JASMINE: I named him Charlie. And the funny thing is that he croaked after only a couple of days.

MOM: Then her fish died and I thought, what am I going to do now? She never knew this, but I bought a replacement fish so she wouldn't feel sad.

JASMINE: She thought I never knew this, but Mom snuck off to the store and replaced Charlie with Charlie Number Two. I fed him every morning before school. I loved that fish. Stupid, huh?

MOM: Yes, we had some great times. But then when I saw her changing... I didn't know what to do. I talked till I had no more words. I cried till I had no more tears.

JASMINE: But my question is this. Why doesn't she stop and listen to me? She listens to everyone else. I want her to understand and accept me for who I am.

MOM: Maybe I didn't want to face the truth.

JASMINE: What's that saying? "The truth shall set you free."

MOM: I don't believe that saying, "The truth shall set you free."

JASMINE: I'm free. That's why I want to get a flag tattoo on my wrist.

MOM: I wonder how she feels.

JASMINE: But no matter what... whatever my mom thinks of me... I still love her. She's my mother.

MOM: Because no matter what... I still love her. She's my daughter. *(MOM and JASMINE turn to face each other. They meet CENTER STAGE and EXIT together.)*

◢◣

WHAT YOU SEE IS WHAT YOU GET
⟫⟫⟫ Jasmine's Monologue ⟫⟫⟫

JASMINE is in her early 20s and wears baggy jeans, a men's shirt, and a ball cap turned backwards.

I never liked dresses and bows. Mom never understood where I was coming from. I think she tried, but only from the viewpoint that if she could understand me, then she could change me. I'd tell her, "Mom, quit trying to turn me into some prissy little girl, because it's not going to happen." *(Pulls on her ball cap.)* I'm not changing for anyone. What you see is what you get. I have plenty of guy friends, but that's all they are—friends. Once Mom tried to push me towards this boy at church. It wasn't a pretty sight. You could call it a slight explosion. *(Yells.)* "Stop it! Stop telling me what to do! Why do you do this?! Why do you always try to force me to do something that I don't want to do? How would you like it? Huh? How would you like it?" *(With a sudden thought.)* "And you already talked to his mom? The two of you set this up? This is so embarrassing! I will never forgive you! Do you hear me? I will never forgive you! I'm not asking him to that stupid dance! I hate him! And I hate you too!"

Carl was nice enough, but he wasn't really my type, if you know what I mean. Now, if Carl was named "Carla," then I might have been interested in going to the dance. You could say I've been like this forever. As a kid, I didn't like Barbie dolls or pink. I'd much rather play with toy trucks or catch spiders in the yard. It's just who I was, but Mom thought she could change me. Like, she would paint my fingernails, and I hated it. I like fingernail polish now... *(Smiles.)* ...if it's black.

Bottom line is... she's embarrassed. Embarrassed that I like baggy jeans, flannel shirts, and short hair. So what? Who's ashamed of their own child? My mom, that's who. She wanted a daughter who was a girly girl. But that's not what she got, is it? *(Pulls on her ball cap.)* Even though my name's Jasmine, that's not what most people call me. You know what they call girls like me. But I don't care. Yeah... I get called a lot of names. Lesbo. Dyke. Butch. Just to name a few. Whatever. *(Pulls on her ball cap.)* Like I said, what you see is what you get.

My mom thinks I'm horrible. I wonder if my mom could even say two or three nice things about me. She couldn't say patience is one of my virtues. You get in my face, I'll get right back in yours. *(Steps forward.)* "You want to mess with me? Huh? Do you?" And I smoke. Mom would be heartbroken if she knew this. So I sneak my cigarettes and use mouthwash. I mean, why give her one more reason to be disappointed in me? Here's another thing she doesn't know… I have three tattoos. All hidden of course. Seems like I hide a lot of things from my mom, huh? Anyway, there's a peace sign. *(Points somewhere on her body.)* It's right here. And a cross… *(Points.)* …right here. And last but not least… right here… *(Points.)* …a lighthouse. I like lighthouses. Maybe it's from all those jigsaw puzzles I used to put together. I'm thinking about getting another tattoo. I want to get an American flag. For freedom. Yeah. *(Indicates her wrist.)* I'd like to put that one right here. Of course, my mom would see it then. *(Shrugs.)* But it's an expression of freedom. That I'm free to be myself.

My mom's always looking for an excuse for me. A reason. Something to put her finger on. My mom blames my lack of having a father for, as she says, my behavior. Yes, *(Air quotes.)* "my behavior." It sounds like I have some sort of mental illness, doesn't it? As if I could just take a daily pill to correct my shameful, unmentionable actions. In my mom's world, it's the absent father's fault. "Oh, father, where art thou?" My parents divorced when I was three. My father was rarely around. Mom would like to blame that, but… *(Shakes head.)* She's just looking for an excuse. To her, the only other possible explanation for me shunning any and all aspects of femininity is her worst nightmare.

But the truth of the matter is… it's nobody's fault. I found my way here all by myself. It's called being me. How simple a statement is that? Being me. Find yourself and be yourself. Rocket science? I don't think so. I like girls. That's all there is to it. It's like, "Can we all be honest here?"

Or what if we all sang that Barney song? *(Or change to a current preschool character that teaches acceptance.)* Something about you loving me and me loving you and in the end, we're a happy family? Isn't that what Barney taught us? So why didn't we all grow up to be more open-minded? Didn't we all watch Barney?

I know my mom is thinking, "If only I could change her." But she can't. Now I'm not saying she's a terrible mother. I could easily say three nice things about her. You bet I could. One. She keeps a nice house. I don't especially like clutter, and she's good at organization and tidiness. Two. She's a friendly person. Everyone who comes in contact with her leaves feeling better about themselves. And she smiles at people and hugs them. She even looks into their eyes and truly listens. *(Shrugs.)* Well, except to me. So there's two. Three. She can be a lot of fun. At least... at least she used to be a lot of fun.

What mom would throw a hundred rings at soda bottles to win her kid a goldfish? My mom, that's who. *(Laughs.)* She was crazy. When I was a little kid, we went to this fair. Fifty dollars later, I was carrying around a goldfish in a plastic bag. I was so happy. I named him Charlie. And the funny thing is that he croaked after only a couple of days. She thought I never knew this, but Mom snuck off to the store and replaced Charlie with Charlie Number Two. I fed him every morning before school. I loved that fish. Stupid, huh?

But my question is this. Why doesn't she stop and listen to me? She listens to everyone else. I want her to understand and accept me for who I am. What's that saying? "The truth shall set you free." I'm free. That's why I want to get a flag tattoo on my wrist.

But no matter what... whatever my mom thinks of me... I still love her. She's my mother.

WHAT YOU SEE IS WHAT YOU GET
➤➤➤ Mom's Monologue ➤➤➤

MOM is in her 40s and wears a conservative dress.

I always put my daughter in pretty little dresses with matching bows. Pink. Especially pink. But in middle school, everything changed. That's when she started acting like... a boy. At first I thought she was just going through a phase. You know, a tomboy phase. I thought surely it would pass. But after a while, I really became concerned. She didn't seem to like boys. Gently—very gently—I encouraged her to like this boy named Carl. He was in the youth group at church. So nice. And good looking too. I told her, "If I were your age, that's the boy I'd have a crush on."

One day, I suggested she ask Carl to the Sadie Hawkins dance. You know, that dance where the girls ask the boys. I even talked to Carl's mom to make sure he wasn't already going with somebody else. Well, you should have seen my daughter's reaction. You'd think I had suggested she sign up for Girl Scouts. Well, I did that too, but that was a different fit of its own. Believe me, she made sure I was sorry I ever suggested the dance with Carl.

She's not at all interested in going out with boys. If only I could put my finger on what caused her to turn out like this. She never did exhibit any feminine qualities. Not in any way. Believe me, I tried to steer her toward feminine things. Like when she was a little girl, I would paint her fingernails pink. But she would glare at her nails and scrape off every bit of the polish.

Bottom line is... I'm embarrassed. I have a beautiful daughter who dresses and acts like a boy. I mean, it's hard for me to admit this, but... I'm ashamed to call her my daughter. I want a daughter I can be friends with. Every so often have one of those mother-daughter days. You know, get pedicures, go shopping, giggle about our celebrity crushes. *(Smiles.)* I've always loved her name. Jasmine Marie. Isn't that a pretty name? But that's not what most people call her. At least under their breath. You know what they call girls like her. But she doesn't care. At least that's what she says.

I believe there are two different kinds of people in the world. You're either one or the other. A man or a woman. If you're born a man, then you should act like a man. If you're born a woman, then you should act like a woman. I used to wonder if my daughter could've been switched at birth. Maybe I almost wished she had been. Does that make me a horrible person?

Not that she's horrible. After all, she does have some wonderful qualities. Like puzzles! She's very good at putting jigsaw puzzles together. Dump a thousand pieces on the table, and she will work on it for hours on end. Then a few days later, you walk into the room and what was once a pile of little cardboard pieces is now a beautiful lighthouse on the shore. You know, not everyone has such patience. And something else. She doesn't smoke. And no tattoos! Thank goodness she doesn't have a tattoo. See? That's three good things about her.

So, here's what I think happened. She needed a father. She needed that male influence in her life. So to compensate... well, you know. If it's not that, then... then it's me. Yes, me. My fault. I mean, what if my over-the-top expectations for lady-like behavior caused this? Demanding she wear those frilly dresses even when she rebelled, forcing her to sleep in curlers, insisting on tea parties and ballet classes? Ignoring her love of trucks and dinosaurs, only to buy her one more pink dress? What if I caused this? So, yes, I blame myself.

And in all honesty... I'm heartbroken. If only I knew for sure what caused her to turn out like she did. Her lack of a father figure... or me? If only I could change her. If only... if only there was a magic button, a re-do, an undo, or a backspace key. Does that make me a terrible mother?

I didn't start out terrible. *(Laughs.)* Oh, I remember this time when she was five or six years old, and we went to the county fair. She wanted a goldfish, and I was determined to win her one. "Ten rings for five dollars? Sure, I can do this." *(As if tossing a ring.)* "Come on! Come on! Get on there!" *(Looks down as if talking to a younger Jasmine.)* "Watch this! I'm going to make it this time!" *(Leans forward, tosses another ring.)* "Missed again?" *(As if speaking to the carnival person.)* "Give me ten more rings." *(To a younger Jasmine.)* "I'm going to do it this time. I know! Maybe if I do something crazy. Watch this! I'm going to turn my back, close my eyes, and land this silly ring on that bottle!" *(Turns around, closes her eyes and tosses.)* "There!" *(Pause.)* "What? I did it?" *(Turns back around.)* "I really did it?" *(Laughing.)* "Look at that! Your mother just won you a goldfish! Did you see that?" *(Looking down.)* "What are you going to name him?" Then her fish died and I thought, what am I going to do now? She never knew this, but I bought a replacement fish so she wouldn't feel sad.

Yes, we had some great times. But then when I saw her changing… I didn't know what to do. I talked till I had no more words. I cried till I had no more tears. Maybe I didn't want to face the truth. I don't believe that saying, "The truth shall set you free."

I wonder how she feels. Because no matter what… I still love her. She's my daughter.